The Colorado River in Grand Canyon

A River Runner's Map and Guide to its Natural and Human History

Larry Stevens

Front Cover Photo: ©Kristen Caldon / Whitmore view
Back Cover Photo: ©Margeaux Bestard
Design: Mary Williams Design, Flagstaff, AZ
Printing: Ram Offset Lithographers, White City, OR

4rd Printing 2017

Library of Congress Control Number: 2013945118
ISBN 9780615842806

Disclaimer

Users of this river guide do so at their own risk. Neither
the publisher nor the author assumes any liability
related to the use of this guide. Readers are advised to
use their powers of observation and common sense in
all activities in Grand Canyon.

TABLE OF CONTENTS

Preface		4
I: **Maps of the River Corridor**		(7-54)
II: **Geography**		55
III: **Geology**		67
	Geologic History of Grand Canyon	67
	The Colorado River and the Past 75 Million Years	80
IV: **Human History**		87
	History Timeline	88
	Conservation History	94
V: **Biology and Ecology**		97
VI: **Glen Canyon Dam and River Stewardship**		121
VII: **Resources for River Runners**		136
Trail Maps		139
Index		142

References cited in this guide are available on the Grand Canyon
Wildlands website: GrandCanyonWildlands.org

Dedication

This book is dedicated to those who love Grand Canyon, who work on, in, and for the well-being of this extraordinary landscape and its natural, socio-cultural, and spiritual resources.

Acknowledgements

This book would not have been possible without the support and encouragement of my parents, Lorry Levine, Susan Bassett, Jeri Ledbetter, and Kelly Burke. The 2013 revision was funded in part by a director's grant from Wilburforce Foundation, Danny Giovale, and Paul Dayton. I much appreciate the materials and assistance provided by the staffs of the following institutions: the Arizona Historical Society, the National Park Service at Grand Canyon, and the Special Collections Library at Northern Arizona University. My deepest gratitude for their insight and writings go to the Canyon's literati: Tina Ayers, Rich Bailowitz, Anna K. Behrensmeyer, George Billingsley, Dean Blinn, Bill Breed, Steve Carothers, Anne Castle, Laura Crossey, Kim Crumbo, Lois Jotter Cutter, Paul Dayton, Brad Dimock, Brian and Dan Dierker, Roz Driscoll, David Garrett, David Gillette, Terry Griswold, Joseph Hazel, R.J. Johnson, R. Roy Johnson, Karl Karlstrom, Matt Kaplinski, David ("Cosmo") Kreamer, Ivo Lucchita, Paul Martin, James Mead, Ted Melis, Eddie McKee, Vicky Meretsky, Tom Myers, Gary Nabhan, Rod Parnell, John Polhemus, Peter Price, Roger Pulwarty, Richard Quartaroli, Glenn Rink, Carl Olson, Vincent Roth, David Rubin, Jack Schmidt, Dan Simberloff, Robert Snow, John Spence, Abe Springer, David Topping, Ray Turner, Richard Valdez, Mike Woodburne, Mike Yard, Gwen Waring, Alton Wasson, Robert Webb, David Wegner, and others. The following people read early versions of the text and made valuable suggestions for which I am also truly grateful: Dave Elliott, Don Elston, George Billingsley and Karl Karlstrom (geology); Lorry Levine and Fred Eiseman (history); Robert Euler (anthropology); Steve Carothers (the dam); Bryan Brown, R. Roy Johnson, Chuck Minckley, Art Phillips and George Ruffner (biology). Any mistakes in this book are those of the author, not of these many fine scholars. We thank the many fine photographers who are credited throughout the guide. Special thanks to Ron Blakey for his paleogeographic reconstructions. My thanks for editorial assistance go to Mary Ellen Arndorfer, Sue Bassett, Kelly Burke, Rich Cifelli, Jocelyn Gibbon, Lynn Hamilton, Tom Myers, Rob Noonan, Richard Quartaroli, Gibby Siemion, Anne Slobodchikoff, and Drifter Smith. Thanks to Mary Williams for map and book design, and Chris Cone and Marguerite Hendrie for figure illustrations. Thanks to Tom Gushue/GCMRC for mapping assistance and data. Special thanks also go to Fred and Alex Thevenin and AzRA for their support of the production and printing of this book.

PREFACE TO THE 2017 EDITION

The gates of Glen Canyon Dam closed 54 years ago, and 34 years have flowed under the Black Bridge at Phantom Ranch since I published the first edition of this guidebook. Revered by Nature pilgrims, and famously over-allocated, the Colorado River in Grand Canyon is now the most carefully studied large, constrained river in the world. Although 50 years would seem enough time for the river to have adjusted to the dam, and for us to understand dam impacts, that simply has not been the case. We continue to learn about the importance of past events, and those of us watching are routinely surprised by the river's changes. Although it is socio-hydrologically shackled and pasted up with a baffling array of political abbreviations, the river ecosystem remains an enormous mystery, a living, changing, multidimensional masterpiece of nature.

The first edition of this book in 1983 emerged during a time of foment in river management. Lake Powell finally filled in 1980. Under the heat of mounting public pressure to improve environmental stewardship in late 1982, Secretary of the Interior James Watt had just initiated the Bureau of Reclamation's Glen Canyon Environmental Studies Program, setting in motion a tsunami of research to better understand the consequences of flow regulation.[274, 323] But the spring of 1983 saw overwhelming runoff into Lake Powell. More than 92,000 cfs (2,622 m^3/s) was released through and around the dam. While only the equivalent of a 2-year springtime peak flow in the predam era, considerable damage occurred to the Dam's spillways and downstream. Unplanned floods, passage of the 1992 Grand Canyon Protection Act, and leadership under David L. Wegner and the subsequent Adaptive Management Program (AMP; and the US Geological Survey Grand Canyon Monitoring and Research Center) have dramatically changed Colorado River politics, science, and management.[308]

The Colorado River carries more politics than water, and its stewardship suffers from societal strabismus: the two eyes of our culture are out of binocular alignment, one focused on the river's future economics and the other focused on its environmental past. The primary product of western appropriative water law is conflict, which is apparent to all who sit through AMP meetings. But in coming to know the many river managers, scientists, and water buffaloes on both sides of the economics-environment coin, I find that most try, within their limits, to do what is best for their constituencies, for society, and for the resources they value. There is always much opportunity for disagreement, but making a sincere effort to understand other's concerns helps us develop consensus in areas of former conflict, as reflected in the recently approved Long Term Experimental Management Plan Environmental Impact Statement (2016).[303]

Over the past 45 years I have been honored to accompany many first-time visitors and hundreds of scientific, social, artistic, and spiritual authorities through Grand Canyon, from private citizens to senators, spider taxonomists to neural network modelers, and Native American elders. I have been struck by the uniqueness of each visitor's perspective. It seems to me that Grand Canyon is a kind of inverted Jungian onion:[87] each layer another dimension that enlarges the previously understood whole, providing lessons increasingly more intricate and grand than previously envisioned. This kind of seeing realigns our understanding and may provide new solutions to the vexing limitations of human nature. Grand Canyon is larger and more multifaceted than any of us can imagine, a portal into wonder and humility. We have not yet begun to plumb its depths, and as with life itself, the more one learns and brings to it, the more vast and enthralling the world around us becomes.

There is a deep cost to the human spirit of failing to recognize the adequacy and richness of this place as it is. I increasingly encounter river runners who say, "Yeah, it

"Excepting when the melting snows send their annual torrents through the avenues to the Colorado, conveying with them sound and motion, these dismal abysses . . . and the arid table-lands that enclose them, are left, as they have been for ages, in unbroken solitude and silence."

Joseph C. Ives 1858

"...Form and color do not exhaust all the divine qualities of the Grand Canyon... It is the land of music. The river thunders in perpetual roar, swelling in floods of music when the storm gods play upon the rocks and fading away in soft and low murmurs when the infinite blue of heaven is unveiled...Mountains of music swell in the rivers, hills of music billow in the creeks, and meadows of music murmur in the rills that ripple over the rocks. Altogether it is a symphony of multitudinous melodies. All this is the music of waters. The adamant foundations of the earth have been wrought into a sublime harp, upon which the clouds of the heavens play with mighty tempests or with gentle showers."

John Wesley Powell 1875[230]

was really an incredible trip, but too bad that it's…(dammed, managed, crowded, over-researched, etc.)." Grand Canyon is good enough, plain and simple. It is a miraculous, direct expression of Earth's history, processes, and biota, a place where, with humility, we can recover ourselves and re-enter a desert Eden. All ground is sacred and should be treated as such, but among landscapes the Canyon is surely a temple.

I think our purpose here is to improve stewardship of the Earth, with compassion and respect for all life, to live with a sense of humor and adventure as we move towards spiritual fulfillment, honoring the memories and spirits of our parents and ancestors, working for the common good, and protecting our natural heritage. If each of us took up, as our life's legacy the protection of one species or one ecosystem we could prevent the looming sixth great extinction. To do so requires hope, resolve, inspiration, and working together. It has been a great joy and an honor to work in Grand Canyon and with those who recognize and attend to its well-being.

Larry Stevens
Flagstaff, Arizona

I. RIVER CORRIDOR MAP

The following maps of the Colorado River corridor in Grand Canyon have been compiled from various sources, as well as from personal experience.

River miles correspond with the most recent USGS-GCMRC measurements.

Rapid ratings are based on a 1 to 10 scale (increasing in difficulty). Ratings are presented in order of four water levels: Very low (1,000 – 3,000 cfs), Low (3,000 – 9,000 cfs), Medium (9,000–16,000 cfs) and High (16,000 – 35,000 cfs). At flows exceeding 35,000 cfs many rapids wash out, but those that increase in severity are marked "+."

Camps include those most commonly used, although many other camps exist, particularly for parties of 10 or fewer.

The English system of river miles is used by convention in Grand Canyon.

Conversions: 1 foot = 30.48 cm; 1 meter = 1.09 yards; 1 mile = 1.609 km, 1 km = 0.62 miles; 1000 ft³/sec = 28.3 m³/sec, 1m³/sec = 35.3 ft³/sec; 1 million ac-ft/yr = 1,381.3 ft³/ sec; 1 ac-ft = 43,560 ft³ = 1233.5 m³.

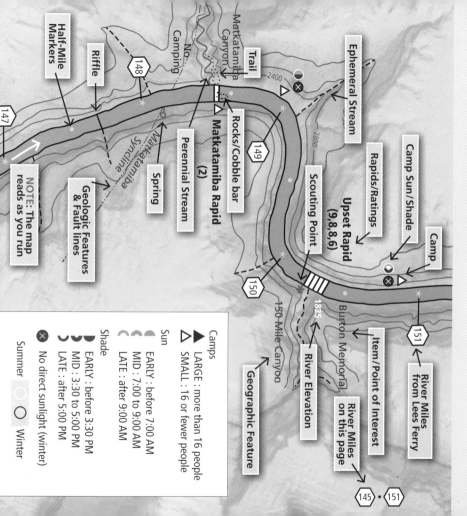

Camps
- ▲ ▶ LARGE : more than 16 people
- △ SMALL : 16 or fewer people

Sun
- EARLY : before 7:00 AM
- MID : 7:00 to 9:00 AM
- LATE : after 9:00 AM

Shade
- EARLY : before 3:30 PM
- MID : 3:30 to 5:00 PM
- LATE : after 5:00 PM

- ⊗ No direct sunlight (winter)
  - Summer
  - Winter

Labels on map:
- Half-Mile Markers
- Riffle
- 148
- No Camping
- Matkatamiba Canyon
- 2400
- Trail
- Ephemeral Stream
- 147
- NOTE: The map reads as you run
- Geologic Features & Fault lines
- Matkatamiba Syncline
- Spring
- Perennial Stream
- Matkatamiba Rapid (2)
- Rocks/Cobble bar
- 149
- 2800
- Rapids/Ratings
- Camp Sun/Shade
- Scouting Point
- Upset Rapid (9,8,8,6)
- 150
- 150-Mile Canyon
- 1825
- Burton Memorial
- River Elevation
- Geographic Feature
- Camp
- 151
- Item/Point of Interest
- River Miles on this page
- River Miles from Lees Ferry
- 145 · 151

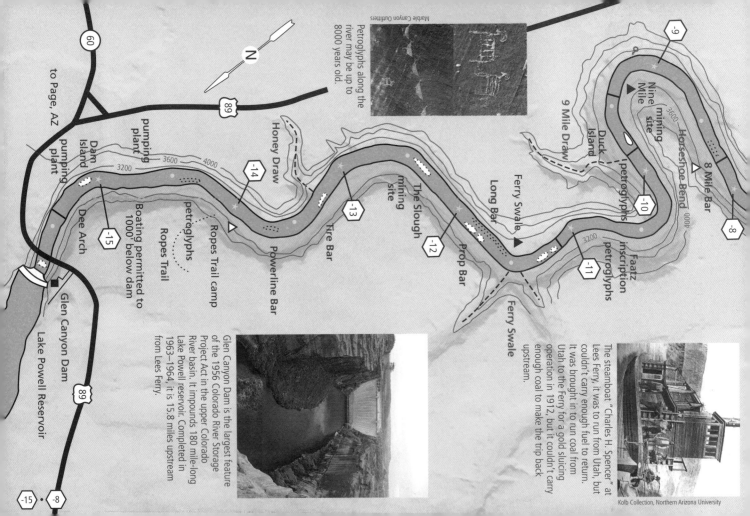

60

89

to Page, AZ

89

N

Petroglyphs along the river may be up to 8000 years old.

Marble Canyon Outfitters

pumping plant
pumping plant
pumping plant

Dam Island

Dee Arch

3200

3600

4000

-15

-14

Boating permitted to 1000' below dam

Ropes Trail camp
petroglyphs
Ropes Trail

Ropes Trail camp petroglyphs

Honey Draw

Powerline Bar

Tire Bar

-13

The Slough mining site

-12

Prop Bar

Long Bar

Ferry Swale

Ferry Swale

-11

Faatz inscription petroglyphs

petroglyphs

3200

Duck Island

9 Mile Draw

Nine Mile mining site

3600

-10

Horseshoe Bend

4000

-9

8 Mile Bar

-8

Glen Canyon Dam

Lake Powell Reservoir

Glen Canyon Dam is the largest feature of the 1956 Colorado River Storage Project Act in the upper Colorado River basin. It impounds 180 mile-long Lake Powell reservoir. Completed in 1963-1964, it is 15.8 miles upstream from Lees Ferry.

The steamboat "Charles H. Spencer" at Lees Ferry, it was to run from Utah, but couldn't carry enough fuel to return. It was brought in to run coal from Utah to the Ferry for a gold sluicing operation in 1912, but it couldn't carry enough coal to make the trip back upstream.

Kolb Collection, Northern Arizona University

-15 • -8

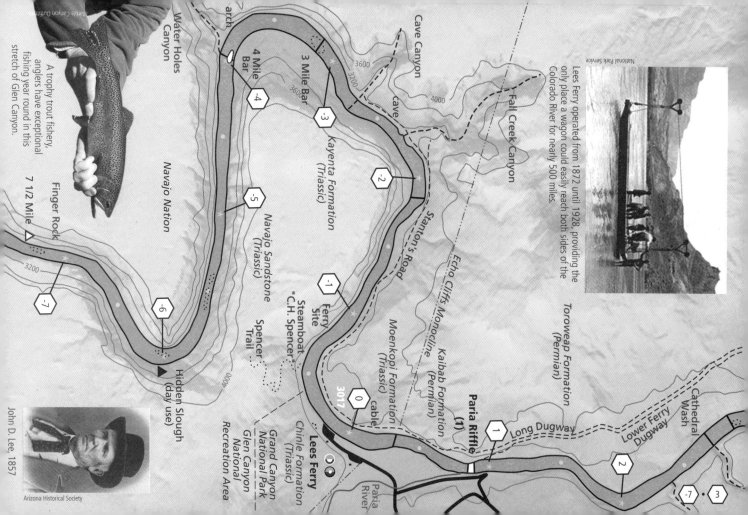

Marble Canyon Outfitters

A trophy trout fishery, anglers have exceptional fishing year round in this stretch of Glen Canyon.

John D. Lee, 1857

Arizona Historical Society

National Park Service

Lees Ferry operated from 1872 until 1928, providing the only place a wagon could easily reach both sides of the Colorado River for nearly 500 miles.

Water Holes Canyon

Navajo Nation

3 Mile Bar

4 Mile Bar

Kayenta Formation (Triassic)

Navajo Sandstone (Triassic)

Spencer Trail

Steamboat "C.H. Spencer"

Ferry Site

Finger Rock

7 1/2 Mile

Hidden Slough (day use)

Cave Canyon

Cave

Fall Creek Canyon

Stanton's Road

Echo Cliffs Monocline

Moenkopi Formation (Triassic)

Kaibab Formation (Permian)

Toroweap Formation (Permian)

cable

Chinle Formation (Triassic)

Grand Canyon National Park

Glen Canyon National Recreation Area

Lees Ferry

Paria River

Paria Riffle

Long Dugway

Lower Ferry Dugway

Cathedral Wash

-7

-6

-5

-4

-3

-2

-1

0

3017

(1)

1

2

3

-7

3600

3200

4000

3600

3200

4000

Crossbedded Coconino Sandstone

Coconino Sandstone (Permian)

4 Mile Wash

The original Navajo Bridge was built in 1929. The new bridge was completed in 1995. They are 490 feet above the river.

Anya Fayler Metcalf

A fern fossil from the Hermit Shale.

National Park Service

Jackass Creek

Badger Creek Rapid (8,7,6,5)

Badger Canyon

89A

5

6

7

8

3075

3600   3200

3600

3200

3

4

Navajo Bridges

landing strip

Marble Canyon, AZ

lodge

5 Mile Wash

Hermit Shale (Permian)

"Graces Point"

6 Mile Wash

Lees Ferry Rd

Otis "Dock" Marston (left), Ed Hudson (right) and crew embark on first motorized downriver run of the Grand Canyon in 1949.

National Park Service

Back from the brink of extinction, California Condors (Gymnogyps californianus) are often seen around Navajo Bridges.

89A

3 • 8

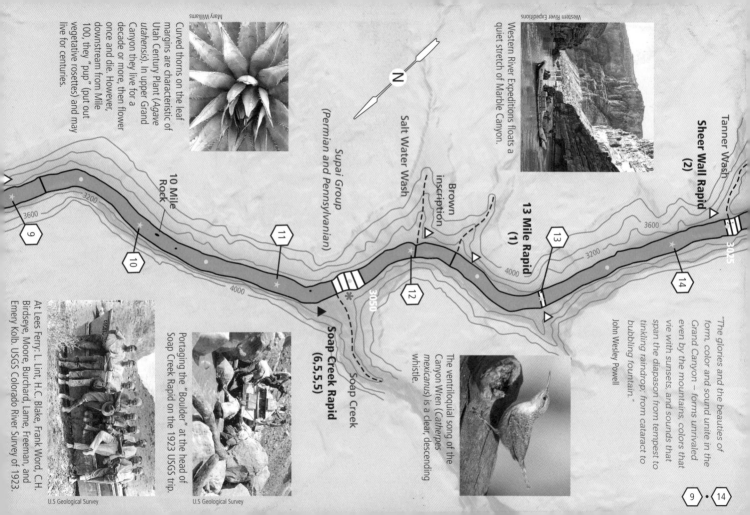

Western River Expeditions floats a quiet stretch of Marble Canyon.

Western River Expeditions

Tanner Wash

Sheer Wall Rapid (2)

13 Mile Rapid (1)

Salt Water Wash

Brown inscription

Supai Group (Permian and Pennsylvanian)

10 Mile Rock

Curved thorns on the leaf margins are characteristic of Utah Century Plant (*Agave utahensis*). In upper Grand Canyon they live for a decade or more, then flower once and die. However, downstream from Mile 100, they "pup" (put out vegetative rosettes) and may live for centuries.

Mary Williams

N

3600

3200

4000

3050

3025

3050

9 10 11 12 13 14

"The glories and the beauties of form, color and sound unite in the Grand Canyon – forms unrivaled even by the mountains, colors that vie with sunsets, and sounds that span the diapason from tempest to tinkling raindrop, from cataract to bubbling fountain."

John Wesley Powell

The ventriloquial song of the Canyon Wren (*Catherpes mexicanus*) is a clear descending whistle.

Soap Creek Rapid (6,5,5)

Soap Creek

Portaging the "Boulder" at the head of Soap Creek Rapid on the 1923 USGS trip.

U.S Geological Survey

At Lees Ferry: L. Lint, H.C. Blake, Frank Word, C.H. Birdseye, Moore, Burchard, Lame, Freeman, and Emery Kolb. USGS Colorado River Survey of 1923.

U.S Geological Survey

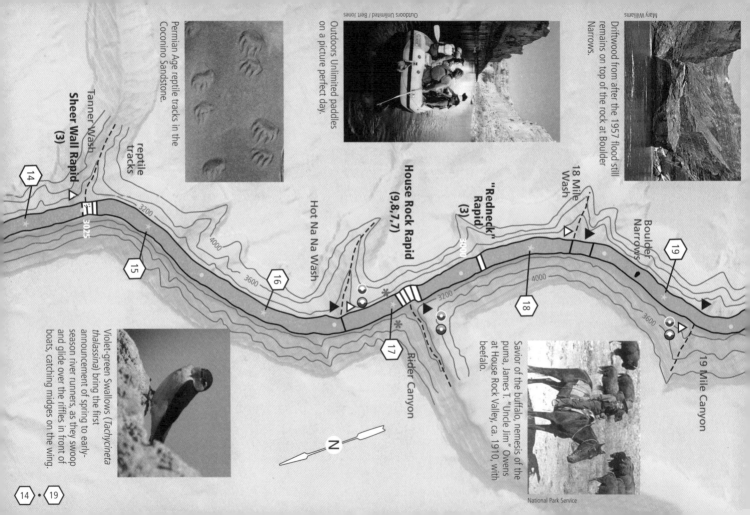

Driftwood from after the 1957 flood still remains on top of the rock at Boulder Narrows.

Outdoors Unlimited paddles on a picture perfect day.

Permian Age reptile tracks in the Coconino Sandstone.

Sheer Wall Rapid (3)

Tanner Wash

reptile tracks

3025

3200

14

15

16

Hot Na Na Wash

3600

4000

House Rock Rapid (9,8,7,7)

"Redneck" Rapid (3)

18 Mile Wash

4000

Boulder Narrows

19

17

18

3200

4000

3600

Rider Canyon

19 Mile Canyon

Violet-green Swallows (*Tachycineta thalassina*) bring the first announcement of spring to early-season river runners, as they swoop and glide over the riffles in front of boats, catching midges on the wing.

Savior of the buffalo, nemesis of the puma, James T. "Uncle Jim" Owens at House Rock Valley, ca. 1910, with beefalo.

N

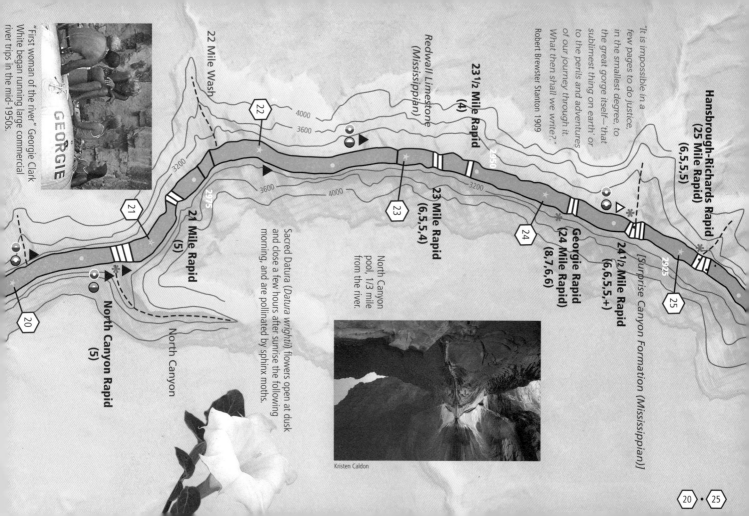

GEORGIE

"First woman of the river" Georgie Clark White began running large commercial river trips in the mid-1950s.

22 Mile Wash

Redwall Limestone (Mississippian)

4000
3600

'It is impossible in a few pages to do justice, in the smallest degree, to the great gorge itself—'that sublimest thing on earth or to the perils and adventures of our journey through it. What then shall we write?'

Robert Brewster Stanton 1909

23 1/2 Mile Rapid (4)

Hansbrough-Richards Rapid (25 Mile Rapid) (6,5,5,5)

2950

3200

[Surprise Canyon Formation (Mississippian)]

2925

24 1/2 Mile Rapid (6,6,5,5,+)

Georgie Rapid (24 Mile Rapid) (8,7,6,6)

23 Mile Rapid (6,5,5,4)

3600
4000

3200

21

22

23

24

25

3200

2975

21 Mile Rapid (5)

North Canyon pool, 1/3 mile from the river.

Sacred Datura (*Datura wrightii*) flowers open at dusk and close a few hours after sunrise the following morning, and are pollinated by sphinx moths.

North Canyon

North Canyon Rapid (5)

20

Kristen Caldon

20 • 25

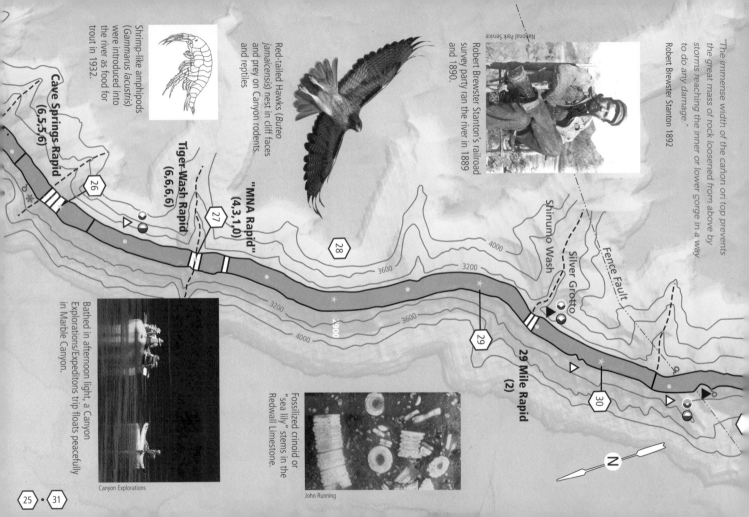

"The immmense width of the cañon on top prevents the great mass of rock loosened from above by storms reaching the inner or lower gorge in a way to do any damage."
Robert Brewster Stanton 1892

Robert Brewster Stanton's railroad survey party ran the river in 1889 and 1890.

National Park Service

Red-tailed Hawks (*Buteo jamaicensis*) nest in cliff faces and prey on Canyon rodents, and reptiles

Shrimp-like amphipods (*Gammarus lacustris*) were introduced into the river as food for trout in 1932.

Cave Springs Rapid (6,5,5,6)

Tiger Wash Rapid (6,6,6,6)

"MNA Rapid" (4,3,1,0)

Shinumo Wash

Silver Grotto

Fence Fault

4000
3600
3200
3200
3600
2900
4000

29 Mile Rapid (2)

Bathed in afternoon light, a Canyon Explorations/Expeditons trip floats peacefully in Marble Canyon.

Canyon Explorations

Fossilized crinoid or "sea lily" stems in the Redwall Limestone.

John Running

26
27
28
29
30

N

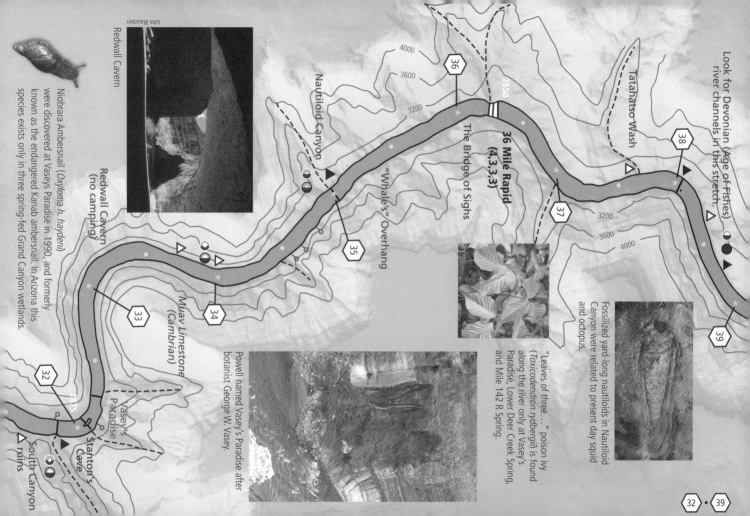

Look for Devonian (age of Fishes) river channels in this stretch.

Tatahatso Wash

36

2850

36 Mile Rapid
(4,3,3,3)

The Bridge of Sighs

38

37

3200

3600

4000

39

Fossilized yard-long nautiloids in Nautiloid Canyon were related to present day squid and octopus.

"Leaves of three . . ." poison ivy (*Toxicodendron rydbergii*) is found along the river only at Vasey's Paradise, Lower Deer Creek Spring, and Mile 142 R Spring.

Nautiloid Canyon

"Whale's" Overhang

35

34

33

Muav Limestone (Cambrian)

Redwall Cavern (no camping)

32

2175

Vasey's Paradise

Powell named Vasey's Paradise after botanist George W. Vasey.

Stanton's Cave

South Canyon
ruins

Redwall Cavern

John Blaustein

Niobrara Ambersnail (*Oxyloma h. hayden*) were discovered at Vaseys Paradise in 1990, and formerly known as the endangered Kanab ambersnail. In Arizona this species exists only in three spring-fed Grand Canyon wetlands.

A Devonian river channel at the contact between the Muav and Redwall Limestones.

Eminence Break

President Harding Rapid (4)

Anasazi Bridge

Point Hansbrough

US Geological Survey

An aerial view of Point Hansbrough. The Point Hansbrough/Eminence Break gooseneck is one of the deepest entrenched meanders in the world.

Bureau of Reclamation proposed Marble Canyon Dam Site tramway site

Redbud Canyon

39

40

41

42

43

44

45

46

47

48

281.5

3600
3200
4000

Buck Farm Canyon

Bert Loper, "the grand old man of the Colorado," died at the oars in 24 1/2 Mile Rapid in 1949.

Bert Loper's boat found here in 1949

Royal Arches

Bert's Canyon

Triple Alcoves

Saddle Canyon

Please use trails in this area

National Park Service

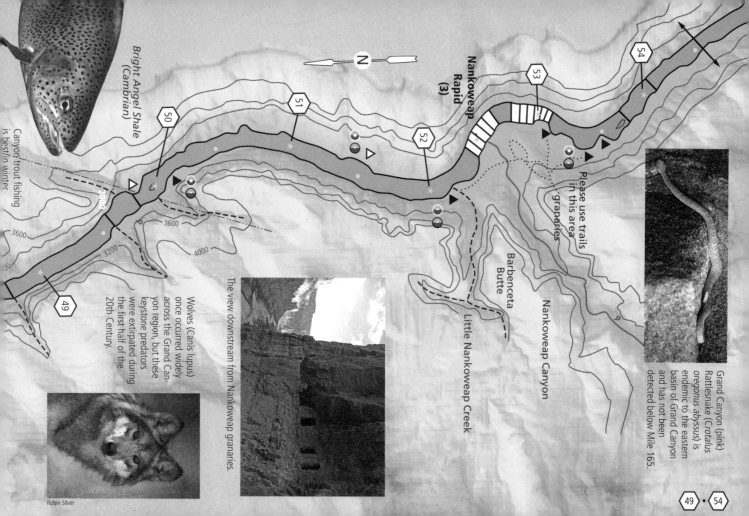

Bright Angel Shale (Cambrian)

Canyon trout fishing is best in winter

N

Nankoweap Rapid (3)

50

51

52

53

54

49

2800

3600

3200

3600

4000

granaries

Please use trails in this area

Barbenceta Butte

Nankoweap Canyon

Little Nankoweap Creek

Grand Canyon (pink) Rattlesnake (*Crotalus oreganus abyssus*) is endemic to the eastern basin of Grand Canyon and has not been detected below Mile 165.

The view downstream from Nankoweap granaries.

Wolves (*Canis lupus*) once occurred widely across the Grand Canyon region, but these keystone predators were extirpated during the first half of the 20th Century.

Robin Silver

49 • 54

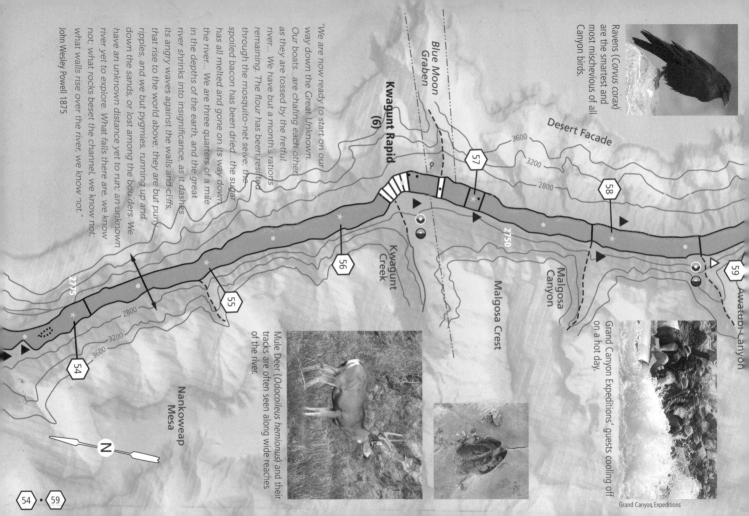

Ravens (*Corvus corax*) are the smartest and most mischevious of all Canyon birds.

Desert Facade

Blue Moon Graben

Kwagunt Rapid (6)

3600
3200
2800

57

58

2750

Kwagunt Creek

Malgosa Canyon

Malgosa Crest

56

55

2775

2800

3200

3600

54

Nankoweap Mesa

N

Awatubi Canyon

59

Grand Canyon Expeditions' guests cooling off on a hot day.

Mule Deer (*Odocoileus hemionus*) and their tracks are often seen along wide reaches of the river.

Grand Canyon Expeditions

"We are now ready to start on our way down the Great Unknown. Our boats...are chafing each other as they are tossed by the fretful river... We have but a month's rations remaining. The flour has been resifted through the mosquito-net seive; the spoiled bacon has been dried...the sugar has all melted and gone on its way down the river... We are three quarters of a mile in the depths of the earth, and the great river shrinks into insignificance, as it dashes its angry waves against the walls and cliffs, that rise to the world above; they are but puny ripples, and we but pygmies, running up and down the sands, or lost among the bouders. We have an unknown distance yet to run, an unknown river yet to explore. What falls there are, we know not; what rocks beset the channel, we know not; what walls rise over the river, we know not."

John Wesley Powell 1875

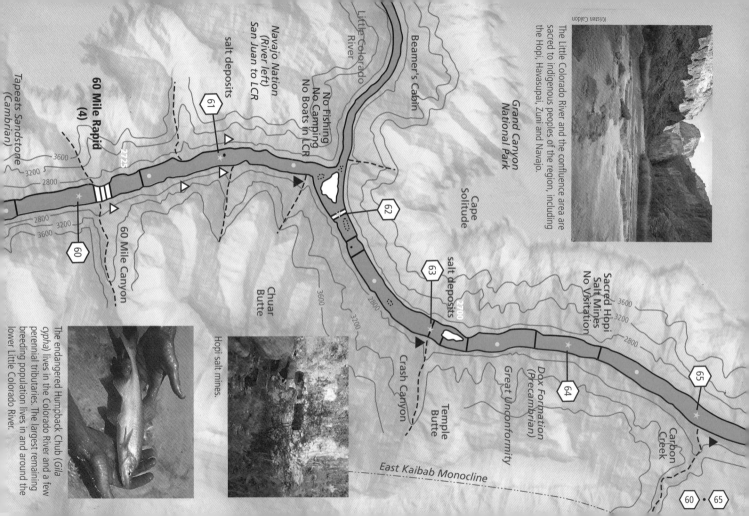

The Little Colorado River and the confluence area are sacred to indigenous peoples of the region, including the Hopi, Havasupai, Zuni and Navajo.

Kristen Caldon

Grand Canyon National Park

Little Colorado River

Beamer's Cabin

Cape Solitude

Navajo Nation (River left) San Juan to LCR

No Fishing No Camping No Boats in LCR

salt deposits

60 Mile Rapid (4)

Tapeats Sandstone (Cambrian)

3600
3200
2800
2800
3200
3600

2725

60 Mile Canyon

60

61

62

Chuar Butte

3600

3200
2800

2700

63

salt deposits

Crash Canyon

Temple Butte

Great Unconformity

Dox Formation (Precambrian)

64

East Kaibab Monocline

Sacred Hopi Salt Mines No Visitation

3600
3200
2800

Carbon Creek

65

The endangered Humpback Chub (Gila cypha) lives in the Colorado River and a few perennial tributaries. The largest remaining breeding population lives in and around the lower Little Colorado River.

Hopi salt mines.

60 • 65

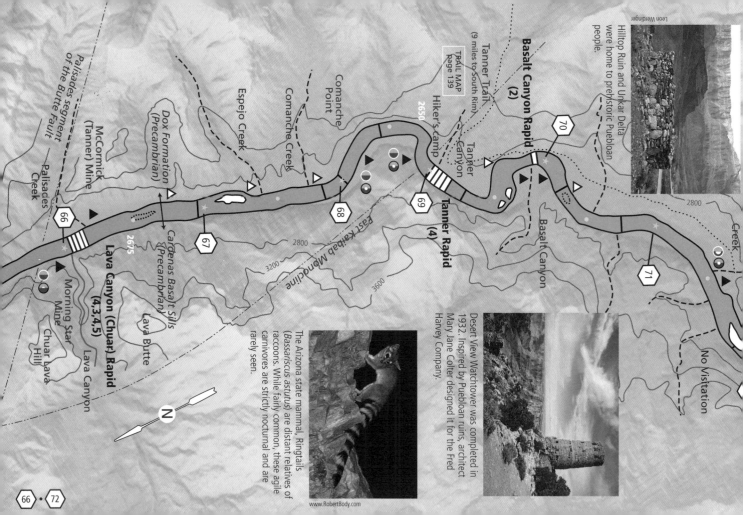

Leon Werdinger

Hilltop Ruin and Unkar Delta were home to prehistoric Puebloan people.

Basalt Canyon Rapid (2)

Tanner Trail (9 miles to South Rim)

TRAIL MAP Page 139

Comanche Point

Espejo Creek

Comanche Creek

2650

Hiker's camp

Tanner Canyon

70

2800

Basalt Canyon

71

No Visitation

... Creek

Palisades of the Butte Fault

Palisades of the Butte Fault segment

McCormick (Tanner) Mine

Dox Formation (Precambrian)

Palisades Creek

66

2675

67

68

East Kaibab Monocline

69

Tanner Rapid (4)

2800

3200

3600

Cardenas Basalt Sills (Precambrian)

Lava Canyon (Chuar) Rapid (4,3,4,5)

Morning Star Mine

Chuar Lava Hill

Lava Butte

Lava Canyon

N

The Arizona state mammal, Ringtails (Bassariscus astutus) are distant relatives of raccoons. While fairly common, these agile carnivores are strictly nocturnal and are rarely seen.

Desert View Watchtower was completed in 1932. Inspired by Puebloan ruins, architect Mary Jane Colter designed it for the Fred Harvey Company.

www.RobertBody.com

66 · 72

Major John Wesley Powell led the first two river expeditions through Grand Canyon in 1869 and 1871–72.

"You cannot see the Grand Canyon in one view, as if it were a changeless spectacle from which a curtain might be lifted, but to see it you have to toil from month to month through its labyrinths."
— John Wesley Powell

A Grand Canyon Whitewater trip approaches Hance Rapid.

Ancestral Puebloans used a *mano* (a handstone) and *metate* (a stone trough) to mill corn and other grains. The Museum of Northern Arizona teamed up with the NPS on excavations along the river near Unkar in the "Grand Archeology" project from 2009–2012.

Unkar Rapid (7,7,6)

granary

Rattlesnake Canyon

ruins

Unkar Creek

Escalante Creek

75 Mile Creek

Papago Creek

Hakatai Shale (Precambrian)

Red Canyon

Escalante Rapid (4)

Shinumo Sandstone (Precambrian)

Nevills Rapid (6)

The Tabernacle

Hance Rapid (10,9,9,8,+)

Spring

spring

73 • 77

74

73

75

76

77

2600
2800
3200
3600
3200
2800
3200
2800
2550

N

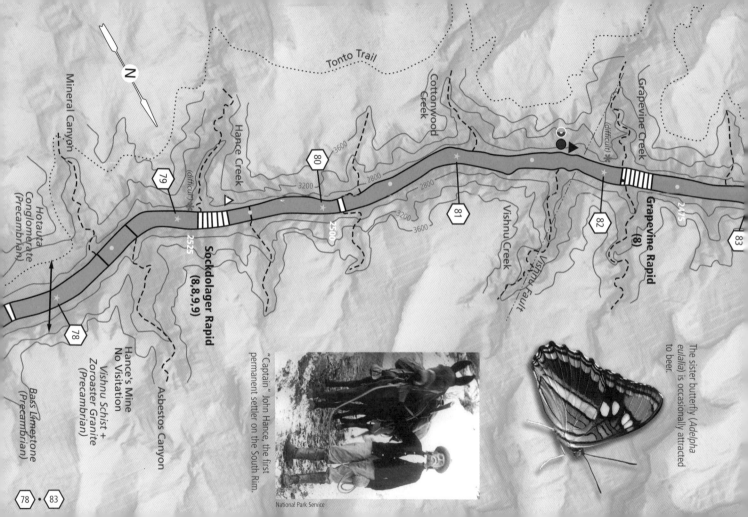

N

Tonto Trail

Cottonwood Creek

Grapevine Creek

Mineral Canyon

Hance Creek

(difficult)

(difficult)

3600

2800

2800

3200

3200

3600

2500

79

80

81

82

83

78

Vishnu Creek

Vishnu Fault

2475

Hotauta Conglomerate (Precambrian)

(difficult)

2525

Sockdolager Rapid (8,8,9)

Grapevine Rapid (8)

Hance's Mine No Visitation

Vishnu Schist + Zoroaster Granite (Precambrian)

Asbestos Canyon

Bass Limestone (Precambrian)

"Captain" John Hance, the first permanent settler on the South Rim.

National Park Service

The sister butterfly (Adelpha eulalia) is occasionally attracted to beer.

78 • 83

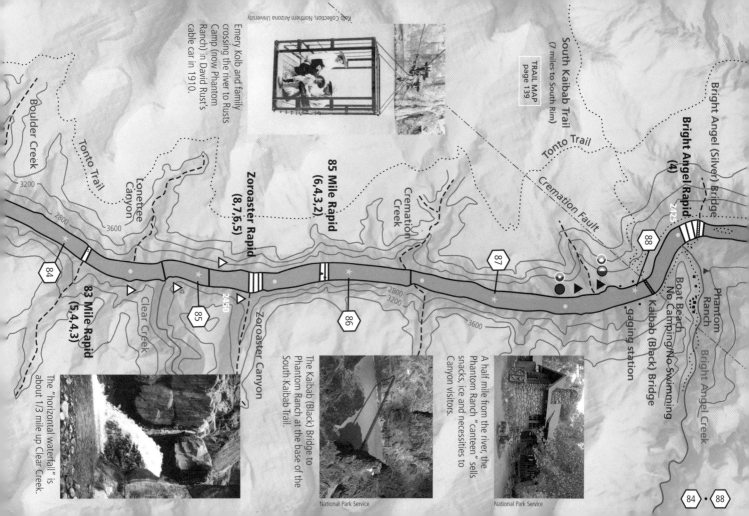

Emery Kolb and family crossing the river to Rusts Camp (now Phantom Ranch) in David Rust's cable car in 1910.

South Kaibab Trail
(7 miles to South Rim)

TRAIL MAP
page 139

Tonto Trail

Cremation Fault

Bright Angel (Silver) Bridge

**Bright Angel Rapid
(4)**

2425

Boulder Creek

3200

Tonto Trail

2800

Lonettee Canyon

3600

85 Mile Rapid
(6,4,3,2)

**Zoroaster Rapid
(8,7,6,5)**

Cremation Creek

87

88

Boat Beach
No Camping/No Swimming

Phantom Ranch

Kaibab (Black) Bridge

gaging station

84

83 Mile Rapid
(5,4,4,3)

85

2450

86

2800
3200

3600

Clear Creek

Zoroaster Canyon

Bright Angel Creek

The Kaibab (Black) Bridge to Phantom Ranch at the base of the South Kaibab Trail.

A half mile from the river, the Phantom Ranch "canteen" sells snacks, ice and necessities to canyon visitors.

The "horizontal waterfall" is about 1/3 mile up Clear Creek.

84 • 88

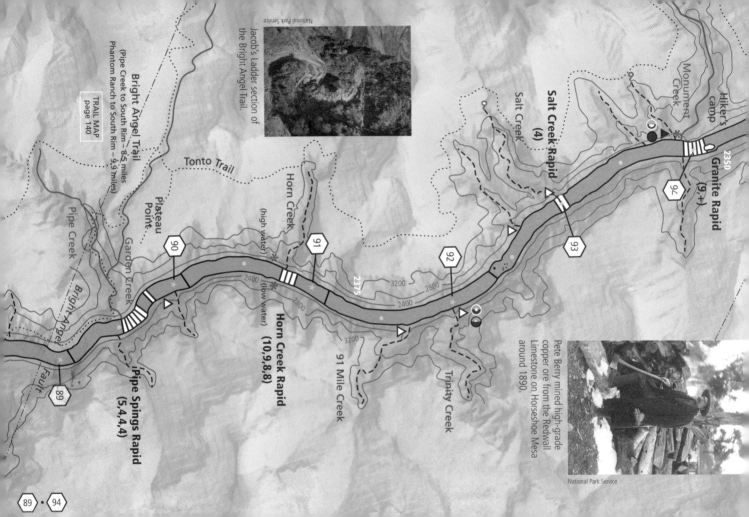

National Park Service

Jacob's Ladder section of the Bright Angel Trail.

Pete Berry mined high-grade copper ore from the Redwall Limestone on Horseshoe Mesa around 1890.

National Park Service

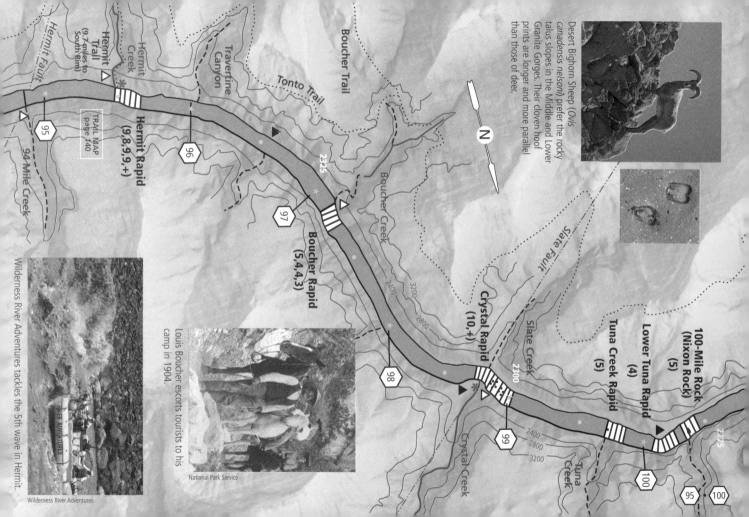

Desert Bighorn Sheep (*Ovis canadensis nelsoni*) prefer the rocky talus slopes in the Middle and Lower Granite Gorges. Their cloven hoof prints are longer and more parallel than those of deer.

N

Hermit Fault

Hermit Creek

Hermit Trail (9.7 miles to South Rim)

Travertine Canyon

Tonto Trail

Boucher Trail

95

94-Mile Creek

96

TRAIL MAP page 40

Hermit Rapid (9,8,9.9,+)

97

Boucher Rapid (5,4,4,3)

Boucher Creek

2225

2400

2800

3200

Slate Fault

Crystal Rapid (10,+)

98

Crystal Creek

Slate Creek

99

3200

2400

2800

3200

100-Mile Rock (Nixon Rock) (5)

Lower Tuna Rapid (5)

Tuna Creek Rapid (4)

Tuna Creek

2225

100

95

100

Wilderness River Adventures tackles the 5th wave in Hermit.

Wilderness River Adventures

Louis Boucher escorts tourists to his camp in 1904.

National Park Service

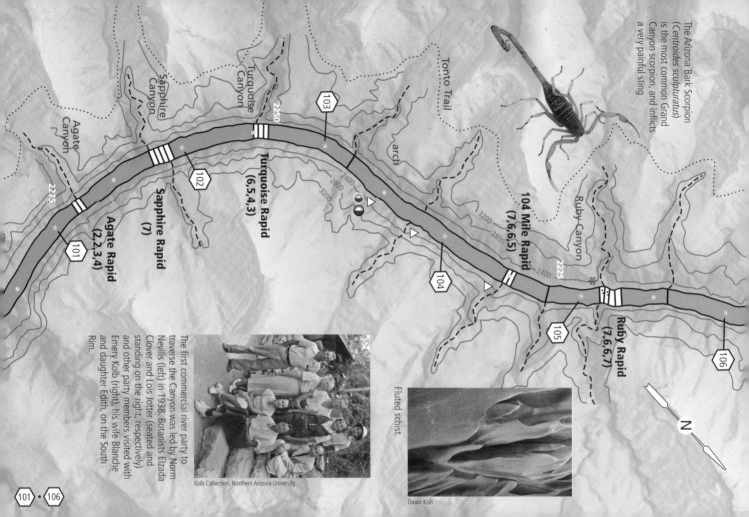

The Arizona Bark Scorpion (*Centroides sculpturatus*) is the most common Grand Canyon scorpion, and inflicts a very painful sting

Tonto Trail

arch

Turquoise Canyon

Sapphire Canyon

Agate Canyon

2250

103

102

2275

101

Turquoise Rapid (6,5,4,3)

Sapphire Rapid (7)

Agate Rapid (2,3,4)

2400
2800
3200

104

104 Mile Rapid (7,6,6,5)

3200
2800
2400

Ruby Canyon

2225

105

Ruby Rapid (7,6,6,7)

106

N

Fluted schist.

Dawn Kish

The first commercial river party to traverse the Canyon was led by Norm Nevills (left) in 1938. Botanists Elzada Clover and Lois Jotter (seated and standing on the right, respectively) and other party members visited with Emery Kolb (right), his wife Blanche and daughter Edith, on the South Rim.

Kolb Collection, Northern Arizona University

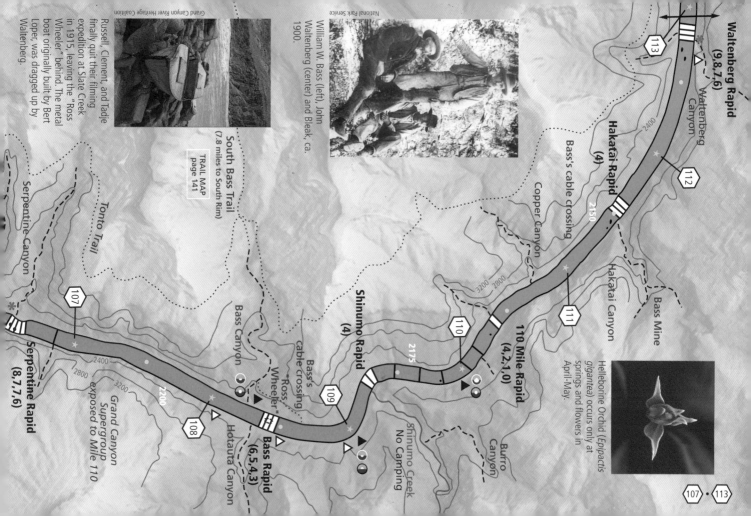

William W. Bass (left), John Waltenberg (center) and Bleak, ca. 1900.

Russell, Clement, and Tadje finally quit their filming expedition at Slate Creek in 1915, leaving the "Ross Wheeler" behind. The metal boat originally built by Bert Loper, was dragged up by Waltenberg.

TRAIL MAP
page 141

South Bass Trail
(7.8 miles to South Rim)

Waltenberg Rapid
(9,8,7,6)

113

112

Waltenberg Canyon

2400

Hakatai Rapid
(4)

2150

Bass's cable crossing

Copper Canyon

3200 2800

Hakatai Canyon

Bass Mine

111

Helleborine Orchid (*Epipactis gigantea*) occurs only at springs and flowers in April-May.

110

110 Mile Rapid
(4,2,1,0)

Burro Canyon

2175

Shinumo Rapid
(4)

109

Shinumo Creek No Camping

Bass Canyon

Bass's cable crossing

"Ross Wheeler"

Bass Rapid
(6,5,4,3)

Hotauta Canyon

Grand Canyon Supergroup exposed to Mile 110

108

Serpentine Canyon

107

Tonto Trail

2400

2800

3200

7200

Serpentine Rapid
(8,7,6)

Elves Chasm

No Camping

117

Royal Arch Creek

arch

2400

2800

3200

116

Monument Fold

Explorer's Monument

Tapeats Sandstone

118

Garnet Canyon

115

113 1/2 Mile Rapid ("Rancid Tuna") (5)

112 1/2 Mile Rapid (6,4,2,1,+)

N

119

STEPHEN AISLE

119-Mile Rapid (4,3,2,1)

Tonto Trail

113

2125

114

2100

119 Mile Creek

120

Waltenberg Rapid (9,8,7,6)

Elves Chasm is a short steep hike from the river at Mile 117.

Maidenhair Ferns (*Adiantum capillus-veneris*) cover the walls of Elves Chasm in Royal Arch Creek.

The Monument Fold meets the river near Mile 116.

Bronze Black

Wayne Ranney

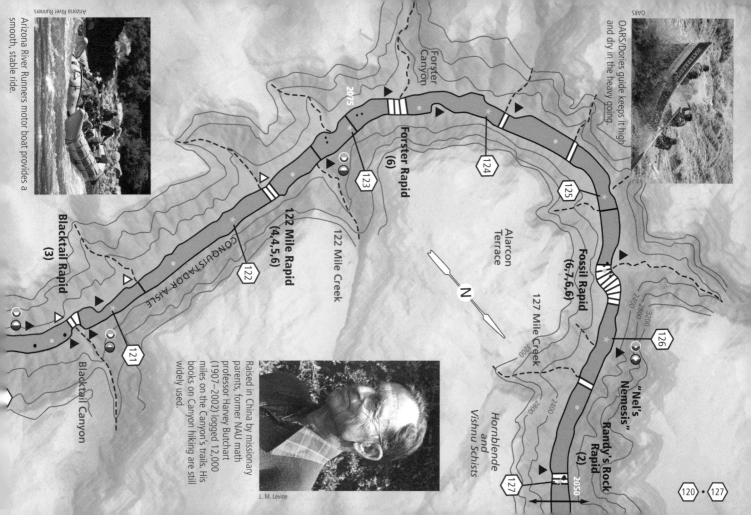

Arizona River Runners motor boat provides a smooth, stable ride.

OARS/Dories guide keeps it high and dry in the heavy going.

Forster Canyon

2075

Forster Rapid
(6)

123

124

125

122 Mile Rapid
(4,4,5,6)

122 Mile Creek

CONQUISTADOR AISLE

122

Blacktail Rapid
(3)

Blacktail Canyon

121

Alarcon Terrace

Fossil Rapid
(6,7,6,6)

127 Mile Creek

3200

3200

2800

2400

2800

2400

2050

126

"Nel's Nemesis"

"Randy's Rock" Rapid
(2)

Hornblende and Vishnu Schists

127

N

Raised in China by missionary parents, former NAU math professor Harvey Butchart (1907–2002) logged 12,000 miles on the Canyon's trails. His books on Canyon hiking are still widely used.

L. M. Levine

120 • 127

Split-twig figurines, made from a single willow twig split down the middle and folded into animal shapes, were found in remote caves in Grand Canyon. Dating back more than 3,000 years ago, they are associated with the Late Archaic hunting and gathering culture.

Even spot-on high-siding in Specter doesn't always prevent a flip.

Bruce Bean

Deubendorff Rapid
(9,8,7,+)

133

1975

132

Bedrock Rapid
(8)

Left run at Bedrock not recommended)

131

Specter Chasm

130

Stone Creek

Galloway Canyon

"Doll's House"

Bass Limestone

Diabase Basalt Sill

2000

2400

2800

3200

Hornblende and Vishnu Schists

3200

2800

2400

MIDDLE GRANITE GORGE

127 Mile Rapid
(4,4,3,2)

129

128 Mile Rapid
(5)

128

Specter Rapid
(8,7,6,5)

Graces Terrace

Specter Terrace

130 Mile Creek

Bedrock Canyon

127 Mile Creek

N

One of many lovely falls along Stone Creek.

Dave Edwards

133/Mile Creek

Tapeats Rapid (8.7, 6.5)

Narrowest point of river — 76 feet wide

Christmas Tree Cave

GRANITE NARROWS

granaries

1925

Doris Rapid (5.6, 6.7)

Deer Creek Slump

1950

(Mind the right wall at high flows)

Bonita Creek Rapid (6.5, 3.3)

135 Mile Rapid "Helicopter Eddy" (5)

Bonita Creek

Bass Limestone over Vishnu Schist

Deer Creek Falls

No Camping

Deer Creek

Dutton Spring

No Camping (at mouth of Tapeats Creek)

Please use trails in this area

Cogswell Butte

Deer Fault

Surprise Valley Trail

N

A view from the river trail into Granite Narrows.

Tapeats Terrace

Tapeats Creek

Upper Tapeats Campground

Thunder River

Thunder Spring

Tapeats Spring/Cave

The spectacular cascades of Thunder River. Its flows are highest in May-June, and Tapeats Creek is subject to summer/fall flash floods.

Crossing Tapeats Creek can be dangerous during spring runoff (May-June)

Crazy Jug

Peter Huntoon

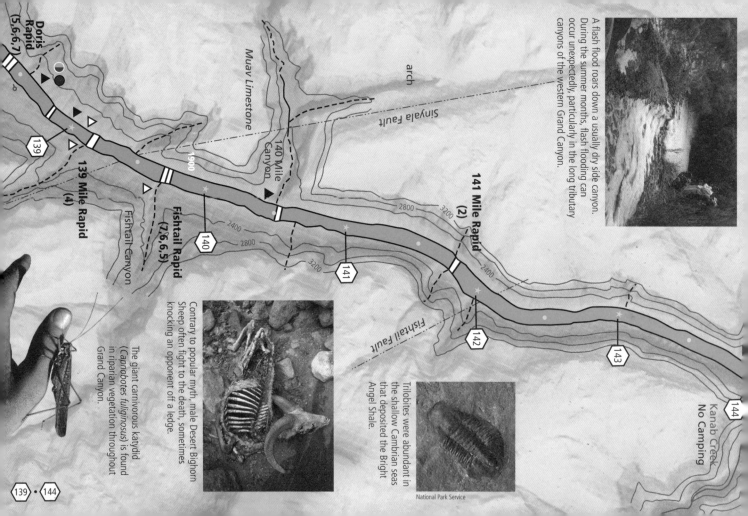

A flash flood roars down a usually dry side canyon. During the summer months, flash flooding can occur unexpectedly, particularly in the long tributary canyons of the western Grand Canyon.

arch

Sinyala Fault

Muav Limestone

140 Mile Canyon

1900

Doris Rapid (5,6,6,7)

139

139 Mile Rapid (4)

Fishtail Canyon

Fishtail Rapid (7,6,6,5)

140

2400

2800

3200

141

141 Mile Rapid (2)

2800

3200

2400

Fishtail Fault

142

143

Kanab Creek No Camping

144

Contrary to popular myth, male Desert Bighorn Sheep often fight to the death, sometimes knocking an opponent off a ledge.

The giant carnivorous katydid (*Capnobotes fuliginosus*) is found in riparian vegetation throughout Grand Canyon.

Trilobites were abundant in the shallow Cambrian seas that deposited the Bright Angel Shale.

National Park Service

139 • 144

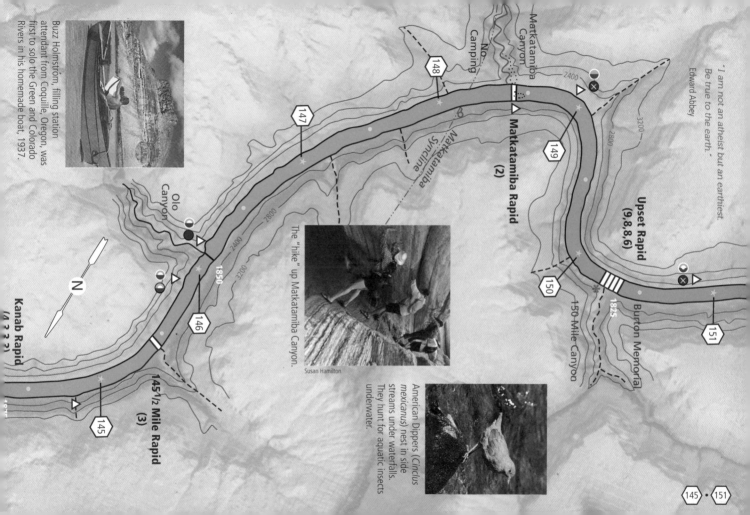

Buzz Holmström, filling station attendant from Coquille, Oregon, was first to solo the Green and Colorado Rivers in his homemade boat, 1937.

Matkatamiba Canyon

No Camping

148

147

Matkatamiba Syncline

Matkatamiba Rapid (2)

149

2400

3200

2800

"I am not an atheist but an earthiest. Be true to the earth."
Edward Abbey

Upset Rapid (9,8,6)

Olo Canyon

The "hike" up Matkatamiba Canyon.

Susan Hamilton

150

150-Mile Canyon

1825

Burton Memorial

151

N

146

2800
3200
2400
1850

Kanab Rapid (6,7,7,3)

145½ Mile Rapid (3)

145

American Dippers (Cinclus mexicanus) nest in side streams under waterfalls. They hunt for aquatic insects underwater.

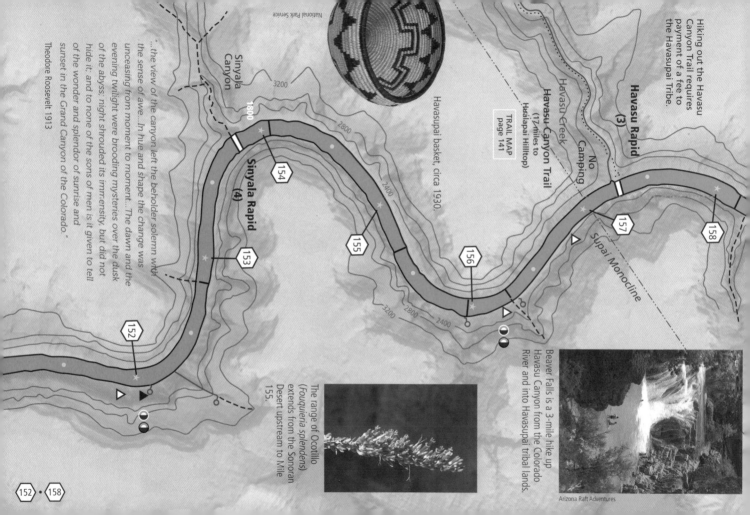

Hiking out the Havasu Canyon Trail requires payment of a fee to the Havasupai Tribe.

Havasu Rapid (3)

Havasu Creek

Havasu Canyon Trail (12 miles to Hualapai Hilltop)

No Camping

Sinyala Canyon

3200

1800

2800

2400

Havasupai basket, circa 1930.

TRAIL MAP page 141

Sinyala Rapid (4)

154

153

152

155

156

157

158

Supai Monocline

2800 — 2400

3200 — 2800 — 2400

"...the view of the canyon left the beholder solemn with the sense of awe...In hue and shape the change was unceasing from moment to moment...The dawn and the evening twilight were brooding mysteries over the dusk of the abyss; night shrouded its immensity, but did not hide it, and to none of the sons of men is it given to tell of the wonder and splendor of sunrise and sunset in the Grand Canyon of the Colorado."
Theodore Roosevelt 1913

The range of Ocotillo (*Fouquieria splendens*) extends from the Sonoran Desert upstream to Mile 155.

Beaver Falls is a 3-mile hike up Havasu Canyon from the Colorado River and into Havasupai tribal lands.

Arizona Raft Adventures

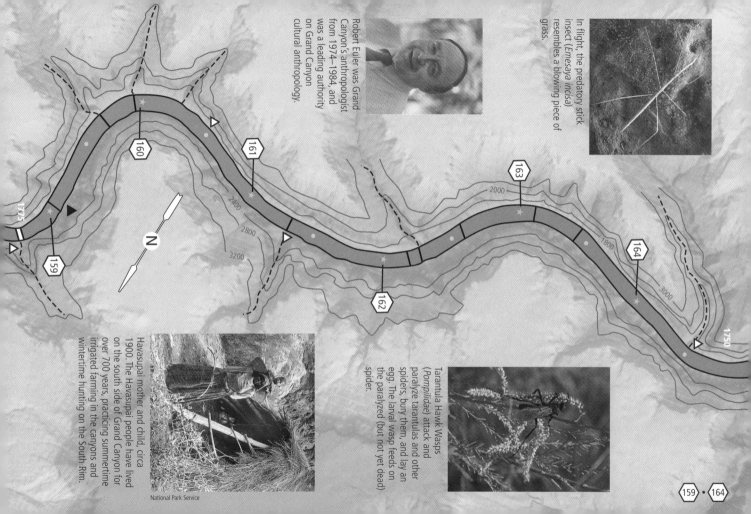

In flight, the predatory stick insect (*Emesaya incisa*) resembles a blowing piece of grass.

Robert Euler was Grand Canyon's anthropologist from 1974–1984, and was a leading authority on Grand Canyon cultural anthropology.

Havasupai mother and child, circa 1900. The Havasupai people have lived on the south side of Grand Canyon for over 700 years, practicing summertime irrigated farming in the canyons and wintertime hunting on the South Rim.

National Park Service

Tarantula Hawk Wasps (*Pompilidae*) attack and paralyze tarantulas and other spiders, bury them, and lay an egg. The larval wasp feeds on the paralyzed (but not yet dead) spider.

N

1775

1750

2000

2400

2800

3200

1800

3000

159

160

161

162

163

164

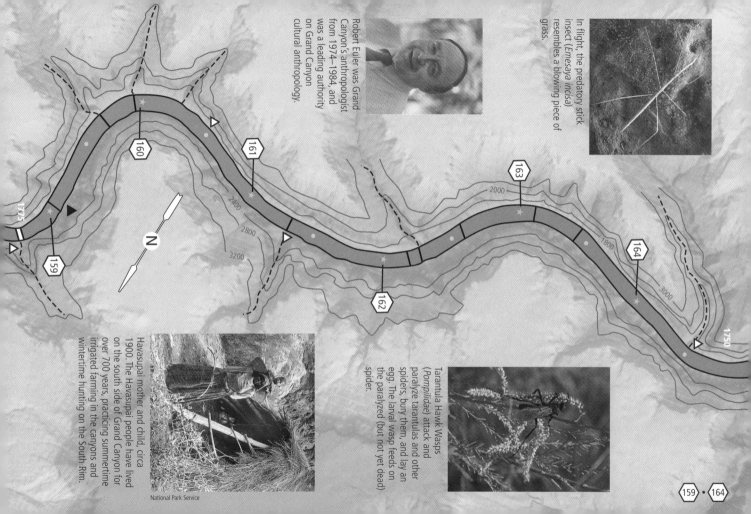

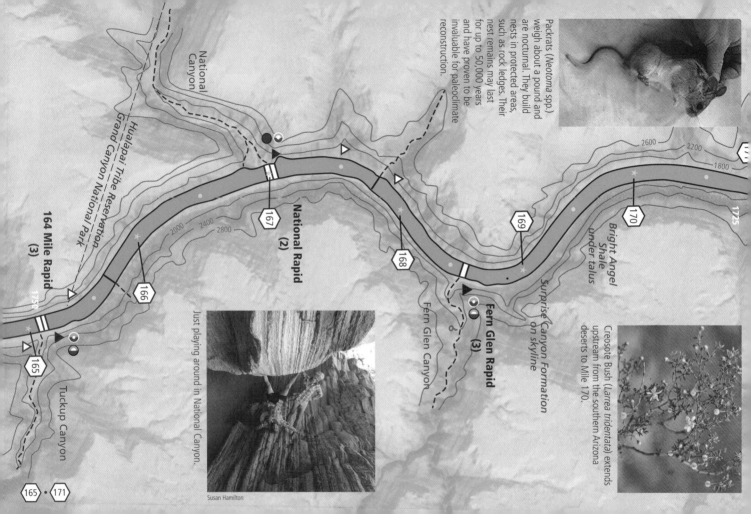

National Canyon

Hualapai Tribe Reservation
Grand Canyon National Park

164 Mile Rapid (3)

166

National Rapid (2)

167

168

169

170

Fern Glen Canyon

Fern Glen Rapid (3)

165

Tuckup Canyon

175V

Surprise Canyon Formation on skyline

Bright Angel Shale under talus

2600
2200
1800
1725

2000
2400
2800

Packrats (Neotoma spp.) weigh about a pound and are nocturnal. They build nests in protected areas, such as rock ledges. Their nest remains may last for up to 50,000 years and have proven to be invaluable for paleoclimate reconstruction.

Creosote Bush (Larrea tridentata) extends upstream from the southern Arizona deserts to Mile 170.

Just playing around in National Canyon.

Susan Hamilton

165 • 171

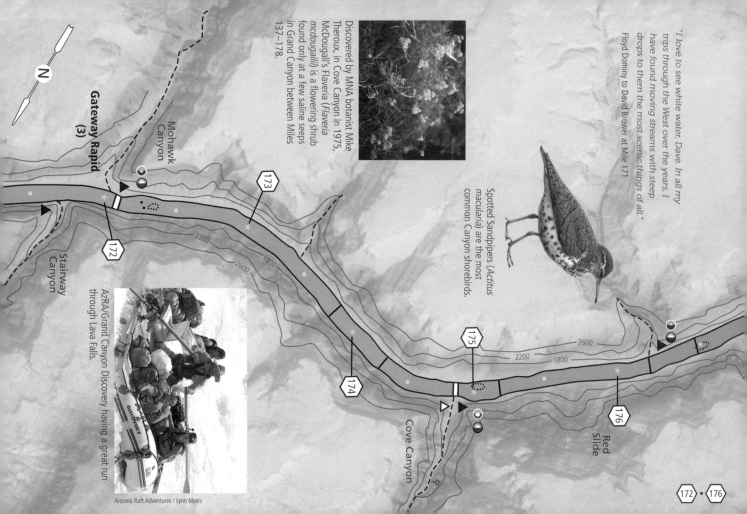

N

Gateway Rapid (3)

Mohawk Canyon

Stairway Canyon

Cove Canyon

Red Slide

173

172

174

175

176

2200

2600

1800

2600

2200

1800

Discovered by MNA botanist Mike Theroux, in Cove Canyon in 1975, McDougall's Flaveria (*Flaveria mcdougalii*) is a flowering shrub found only at a few saline seeps in Grand Canyon between Miles 137–178.

Spotted Sandpipers (*Actitis macularia*) are the most common Canyon shorebirds.

"I love to see white water, Dave. In all my trips through the West over the years, I have found moving streams with steep drops to them the most scenic things of all."
Floyd Dominy to David Brower at Mile 171

AzRA/Grand Canyon Discovery having a great run through Lava Falls.

Arizona Raft Adventures / Lynn Myers

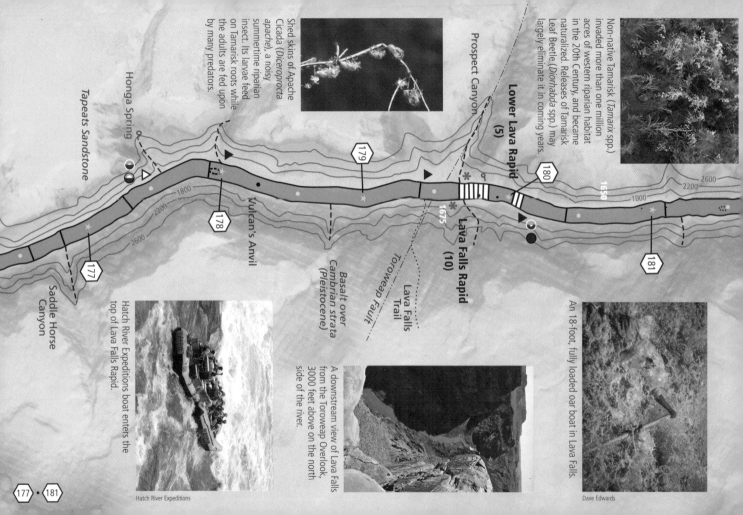

Non-native Tamarisk (*Tamarix* spp.) invaded more than one million acres of western riparian habitat in the 20th Century, and became naturalized. Releases of Tamarisk Leaf Beetle (*Diorhabda* spp.) may largely eliminate it in coming years.

Shed skins of Apache Cicada (*Diceroprocta apache*), a noisy summertime riparian insect. Its larvae feed on Tamarisk roots while the adults are fed upon by many predators.

Prospect Canyon

Lower Lava Rapid (5)

Lava Falls Rapid (10)

Lava Falls Trail

Toroweap Fault

Basalt over Cambrian strata (Pleistocene)

Tapeats Sandstone

Honga Spring

Vulcan's Anvil

Saddle Horse Canyon

177

178

179

180

181

1800

2200

2600

1650

1675

1800

2200

2600

Hatch River Expeditions boat enters the top of Lava Falls Rapid.

Hatch River Expeditions

A downstream view of Lava Falls from the Toroweap Overlook, 3000 feet above on the north side of the river.

An 18-foot, fully loaded oar boat in Lava Falls.

Dave Edwards

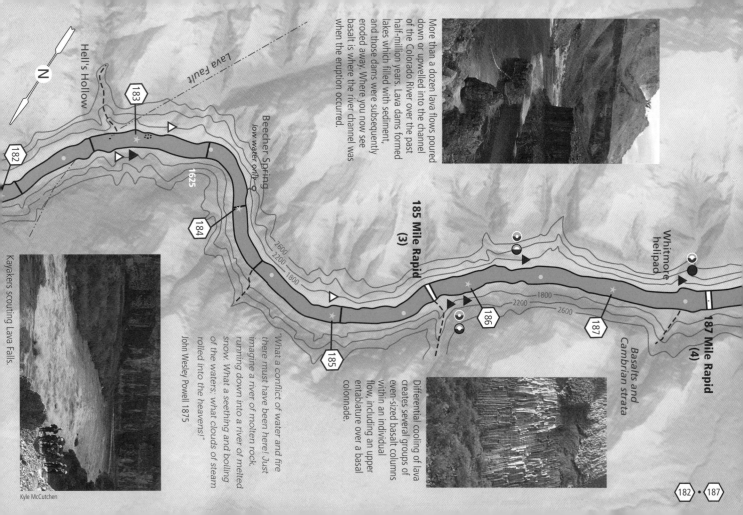

More than a dozen lava flows poured down or upwelled into the channel of the Colorado River over the past half-million years. Lava dams formed lakes which filled with sediment, and those dams were subsequently eroded away. Where you now see basalt is where the river channel was when the eruption occurred.

N

Lava Fault

Hell's Hollow

182

183

184

185 Mile Rapid (3)

186

185

187

187 Mile Rapid (4)

Whitmore helipad

Basalts and Cambrian strata

1625

Beecher Spring
low water only

2600
2200
1800

1800
2200
2600

Differential cooling of lava creates several groups of even-sized basalt columns within an individual flow, including an upper entablature over a basal colonnade.

"What a conflict of water and fire there must have been here! Just imagine a river of molten rock running down into a river of melted snow. What a seething and boiling of the waters; what clouds of steam rolled into the heavens!"

John Wesley Powell 1875

Kayakers scouting Lava Falls.

Kyle McCutchen

182 • 187

Pictographs near Whitmore Wash.

Wayne Ranney

Tapeats
Sandstone
over Schist

191

192 Mile
Canyon

190

1575

192

193

Boulder Wash

193 Mile
Creek

1800
2200
2600

194

N

Staunch opponent of Glen
Canyon Dam and other
dams on the Colorado River,
Martin Litton (1917–2014)
held the record as the
oldest person to row in the
Canyon, at age 92 in 2009.

John Blaustein

Whitmore Rapid
(3)

2000
2400
1800
2200

Hurricane Fault

188

1600

189

Whitmore Wash

Whitmore Trail

188   194

A Tour West trip stops to hike below Whitmore.

Leon Werdinger

Brilliant white Snowy Egrets (*Egreta
thula*) wander the river corridor
throughout the year, but do not nest
here.

194 Mile Canyon

195

Lava cools into a sunburst pattern of fractures along lower temperature flow fronts created by convection.

Charly Heavenrich

Larval antlions or "doodlebugs" (family Myrmeleontidae) dig conical pits in dry sand and wait for their prey. The winged adults are nocturnal and are rarely seen. Larva (top), pits (middle), adult (bottom).

196

Froggy Fault

196 Mile Creek

National Park Service

Lino Gray bowl, from the Basketmaker III, 500-800 AD.

197

198

199

1525

200

201

Parashant Wash

Moki Mac River Expeditions drops into one of the Canyon's many rapids.

Moki Mac

195 • 201

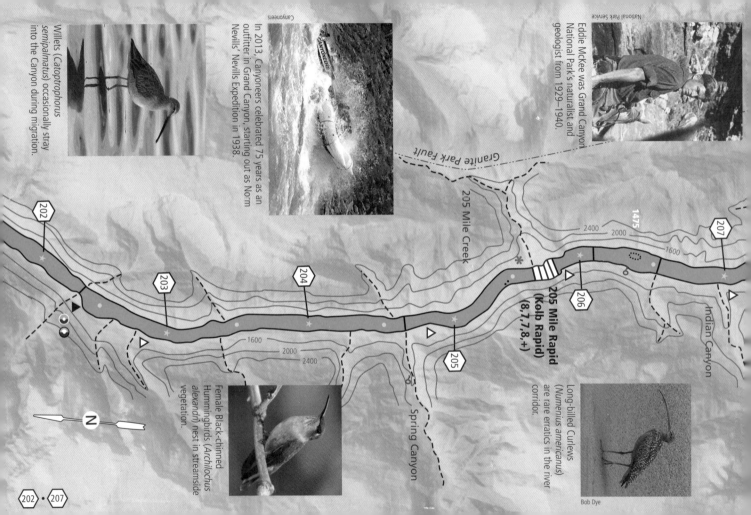

Willets (*Catoptrophorus semipalmatus*) occasionally stray into the Canyon during migration.

In 2013, Canyoneers celebrated 75 years as an outfitter in Grand Canyon, starting out as Norm Nevills' Nevills Expedition in 1938.

Canyoneers

Eddie McKee was Grand Canyon National Park's naturalist and geologist from 1929–1940.

National Park Service

Granite Park Fault

205 Mile Creek

2400
2000
1475
1600

202

207

203

204

205

206

Indian Canyon

205 Mile Rapid (Kolb Rapid) (8,7,7,8,+)

1600
2000
2400

Spring Canyon

Female Black-chinned Hummingbirds (*Archilochus alexandri*) nest in streamside vegetation.

Long-billed Curlews (*Numenius americanus*) are rare erratics in the river corridor.

Bob Dye

N

Turkey Vultures (*Cathartes aura*) may nest in Canyon caves where California Condors and Giant Teratorns nested during the late Pleistocene, 13,000 years ago.

Granite Park

Granite Park Canyon

Hualapai Tribe Reservation

Schist

209

209 Mile Canyon

208

209 Mile Rapid (7)

210

1450

1600

2400

2000

211

Fall Canyon

212

212 Mile Rapid "Little Bastard" (7,5,1)

1425

Pumpkin Springs

213

214

1600

2000

2400

N

Coyotes (*Canis latrans*) are secretive but fairly common in the post-dam Colorado River corridor. They eat lizards, small rodents and mesquite beans, and their crazy jazz howls are occasionally heard on moon-lit nights.

Whipple's Yucca (*Hesperoyucca whipplei*) in the family Asparagaceae lives several to many years and then flowers in March/April, sets seed, and dies.

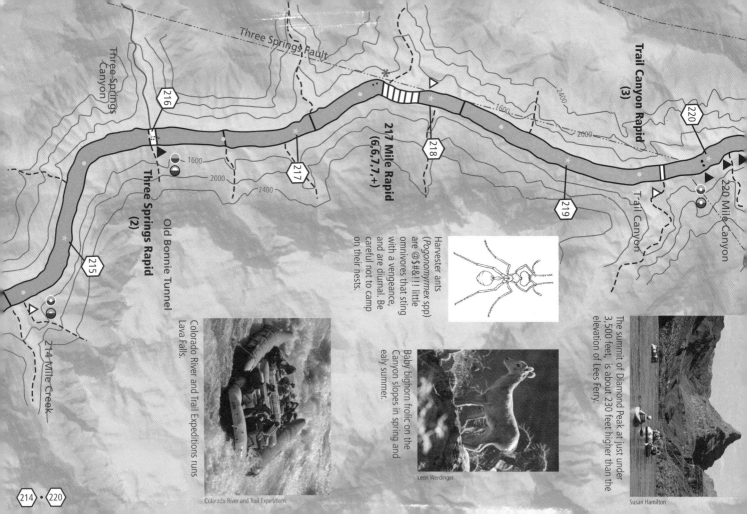

Three Springs Fault

Three Springs Canyon

Trail Canyon Rapid (3)

216

220

1600

2400

2000

218

217 Mile Rapid (6,6,7,7,+)

217

219

220 Mile Canyon

Trail Canyon

1600
2000
2400

Three Springs Rapid (2)

Old Bonnie Tunnel

215

214 Mile Creek

Harvester ants (*Pogonomyrmex* spp) are @$#&!!! little omnivores that sting with a vengeance, and are diurnal. Be careful not to camp on their nests.

Colorado River and Trail Expeditions runs Lava Falls.

Colorado River and Trail Expeditions

Baby bighorn frolic on the Canyon slopes in spring and ealy summer.

Leon Werdinger

The summit of Diamond Peak at just under 3,500 feet, is about 230 feet higher than the elevation of Lees Ferry.

Susan Hamilton

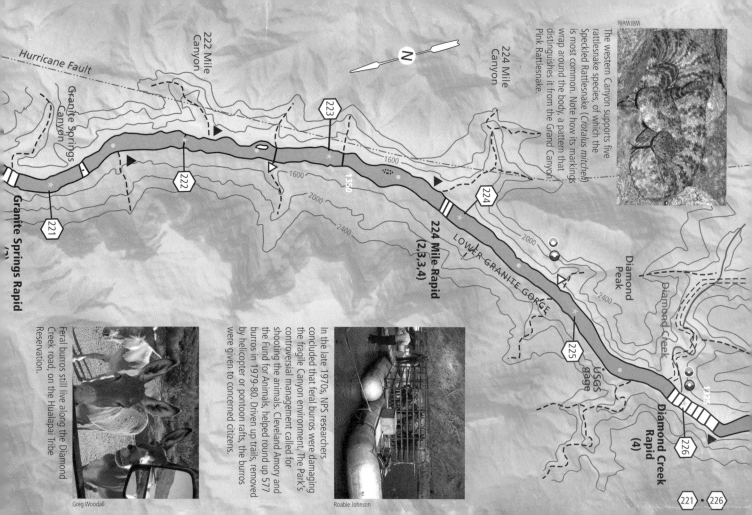

The western Canyon supports five rattlesnake species, of which the Speckled Rattlesnake (*Crotalus mitchelli*) is most common. Note how its markings wrap around the body, a pattern that distinguishes it from the Grand Canyon Pink Rattlesnake.

Will Wells

N

Hurricane Fault

Granite Springs Canyon

222 Mile Canyon

224 Mile Canyon

223

222

224

1600

1600

1350

2000

2400

221

Granite Springs Rapid (3)

224 Mile Rapid (2,3,3,4)

LOWER GRANITE GORGE

2000

Diamond Peak

2400

225

USGS gage

Diamond Creek

1725

Diamond Creek Rapid (4)

226

Feral burros still live along the Diamond Creek road, on the Hualapai Tribe Reservation.

Greg Woodall

In the late 1970s, NPS researchers concluded that feral burros were damaging the fragile Canyon environment. The Park's controversial management called for shooting the animals. Cleveland Amory and the Fund for Animals, helped round up 577 burros in 1979-80. Driven up trails, removed by helicopter or pontoon rafts, the burros were given to concerned citizens.

Roabie Johnson

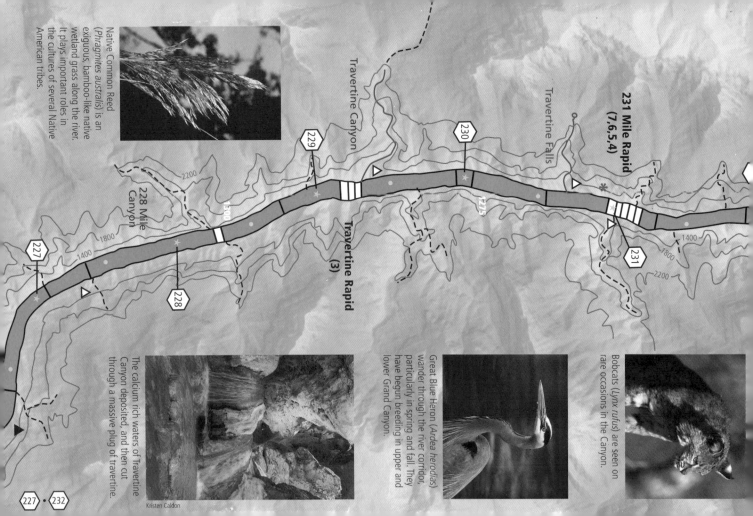

Native Common Reed (*Phragmites australis*) is an exiguous, bamboo-like native wetland grass along the river. It plays important roles in the cultures of several Native American tribes.

228 Mile Canyon

Travertine Canyon

Travertine Rapid (3)

Travertine Falls

231 Mile Rapid (7,6,5,4)

227

228

229

230

231

2200

1300

1800

1400

1275

1400

1800

2200

The calcium rich waters of Travertine Canyon deposited, and then cut through a massive plug of travertine.

Kristen Caldon

Great Blue Heron (*Ardea herodias*) wander through the river corridor, particularly in spring and fall. They have begun breeding in upper and lower Grand Canyon.

Bobcats (*Lynx rufus*) are seen on rare occasions in the Canyon.

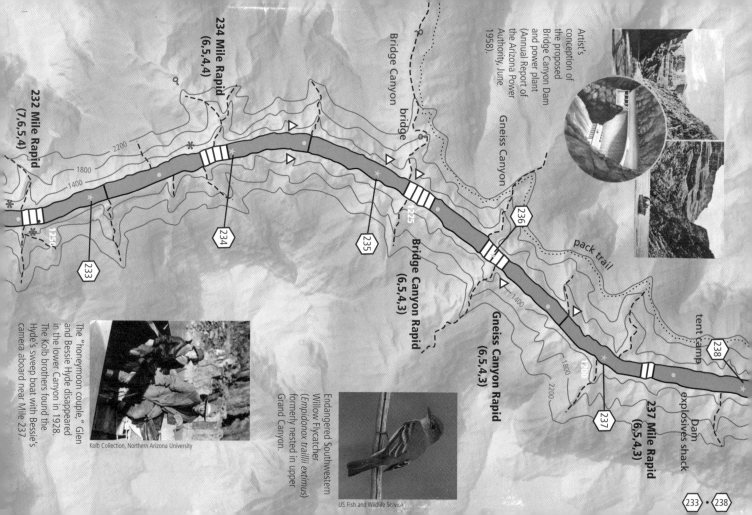

232 Mile Rapid
(7,6,5,4)

234 Mile Rapid
(6,5,4)

Bridge Canyon

bridge

Artist's
conception of
the proposed
Bridge Canyon Dam
and power plant
(Annual Report of
the Arizona Power
Authority, June
1958.

Gneiss Canyon

1250

233

234

235

1225

236

Bridge Canyon Rapid
(6,5,4,3)

Gneiss Canyon Rapid
(6,5,4,3)

pack trail

1400

1200

1800

2200

237

tent camp

238

Dam
explosives shack

237 Mile Rapid
(6,5,4,3)

The "honeymoon couple," Glen
and Bessie Hyde disappeared
in the lower Canyon in 1928.
The Kolb brothers found the
Hyde's sweep boat with Bessie's
camera aboard near Mile 237.

Kolb Collection, Northern Arizona University

Endangered Southwestern
Willow Flycatcher
(*Empidonax traillii extimus*)
formerly nested in upper
Grand Canyon.

US Fish and Wildlife Service

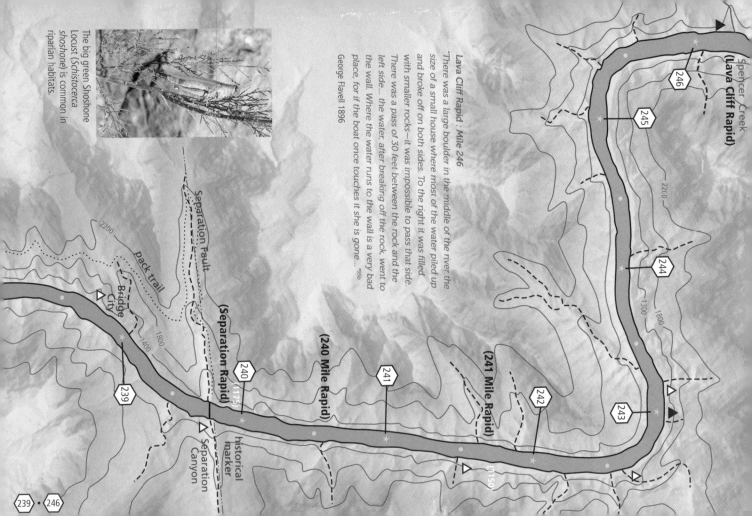

The big green Shoshone Locust (*Schistocerca shoshone*) is common in riparian habitats.

Lava Cliff Rapid : Mile 246

There was a large boulder in the middle of the river the size of a small house where most of the water piled up and broke off on both sides. To the right it was filled with smaller rocks—it was impossible to pass that side. There was a pass of 30 feet between the rock and the left side... the water, after breaking off the rock, went to the wall. Where the water runs to the wall is a very bad place, for if the boat once touches it she is gone...

George Flavell 1896

Spencer Creek
(Lava Cliff Rapid)

246

245

244

2200

2260

1800

1300

243

242

(241 Mile Rapid)

241

(240 Mile Rapid)

240

(117')

(Separation Rapid)

(115')

historical marker

Separation Canyon

Separation Fault

pack trail

Bridge City

2200

1800

1400

239

247 248 247

(Surprise Rapid)

N

Clay-Tank Canyon

1600

1200

2000

Surprise Canyon

249

1175

(Lost Creek Rapid)

250

251

252

1200

1600

2000

Ellsworth and Emery Kolb led the search party for Glen and Bessie Hyde in 1928.

The last Leopard Frog (*Lithobates onca*) in the river corridor was seen in 1990 at the mouth of Surprise Canyon.

Spotted Skunk (*Spilogale gracilis*) are small and rarely seen predators and scavengers.

247 • 252

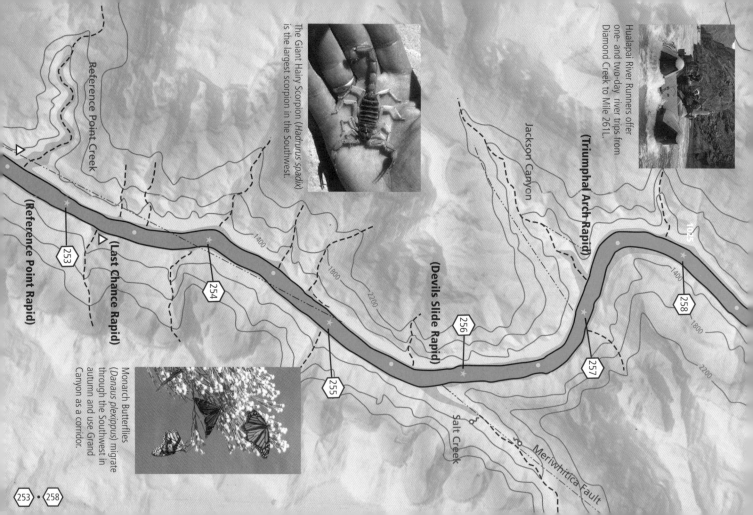

Hualapai River Runners offer one- and two-day river trips from Diamond Creek to Mile 261L.

(Triumphal Arch Rapid)

Jackson Canyon

The Giant Hairy Scorpion (*Hadrurus spadix*) is the largest scorpion in the Southwest.

Reference Point Creek

1400

1800

2200

(Devils Slide Rapid)

(Reference Point Rapid)

253

(Last Chance Rapid)

254

255

256

257

258

1400

1800

2200

1025

Salt Creek

Meriwhitica Fault

Monarch Butterflies (*Danaus plexippus*) migrate through the Southwest in autumn and use Grand Canyon as a corridor.

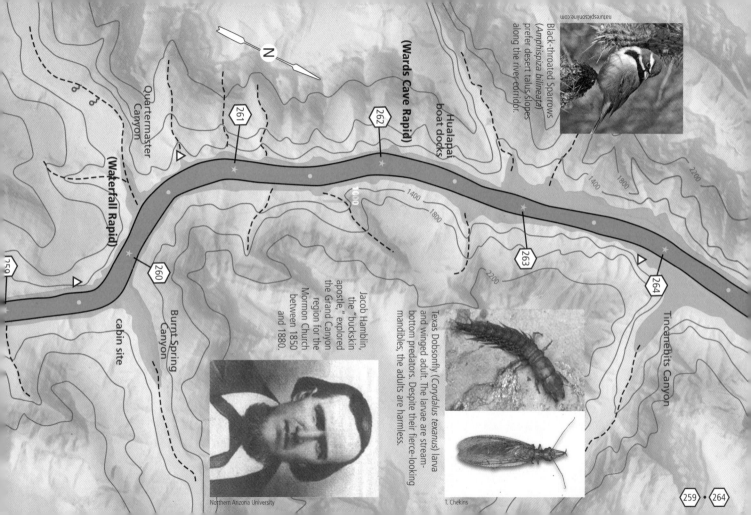

N

Quartermaster Canyon

(Waterfall Rapid)

(Wards Cave Rapid)

Hualapai boat docks

261

262

263

264

260

259

cabin site

Burnt Spring Canyon

Tincanebits Canyon

1000

1400

1800

2200

1400

1800

2200

Black-throated Sparrows (*Amphispiza bilineata*) prefer desert talus slopes along the river corridor.

naturespicsonline.com

Jacob Hamblin, the "buckskin apostle," explored the Grand Canyon region for the Mormon Church between 1850 and 1880.

Northern Arizona University

Texas Dobsonfly (*Corydalus texanus*) larva and winged adult. The larvae are stream-bottom predators. Despite their fierce-looking mandibles, the adults are harmless.

T. Chekins

Shasta ground sloths (*Nothrotheriops
shastensis*) roamed the Canyon until
about 13,000 years ago.

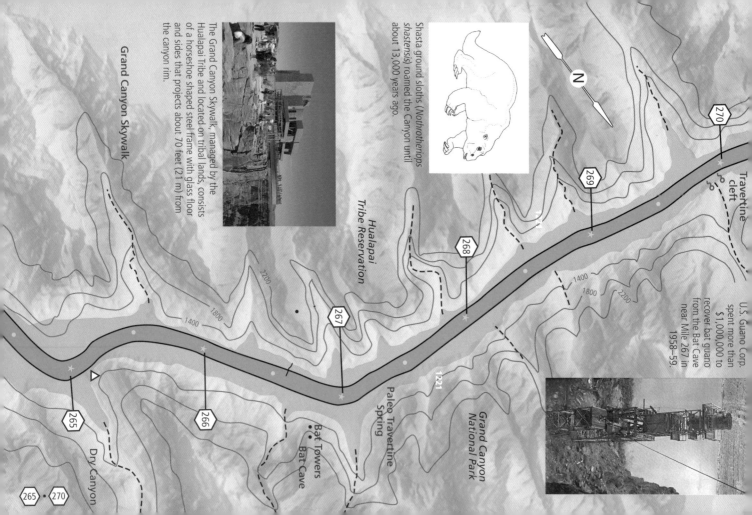

N

270

269

268

267

266

265

Travertine
cleft

U.S. Guano Corp.
spent more than
$1,000,000 to
recover bat guano
from the Bat Cave
near Mile 267 in
1958–59.

Grand Canyon Skywalk

The Grand Canyon Skywalk, managed by the
Hualapai Tribe and located on tribal lands, consists
of a horseshoe shaped steel frame with glass floor
and sides that projects about 70 feet (21 m) from
the canyon rim.

Hualapai
Tribe Reservation

2200

1800

1400

1400

1800

2200

1221

Paleo Travertine
Spring

Grand Canyon
National Park

Bat Towers
Bat Cave

Dry Canyon

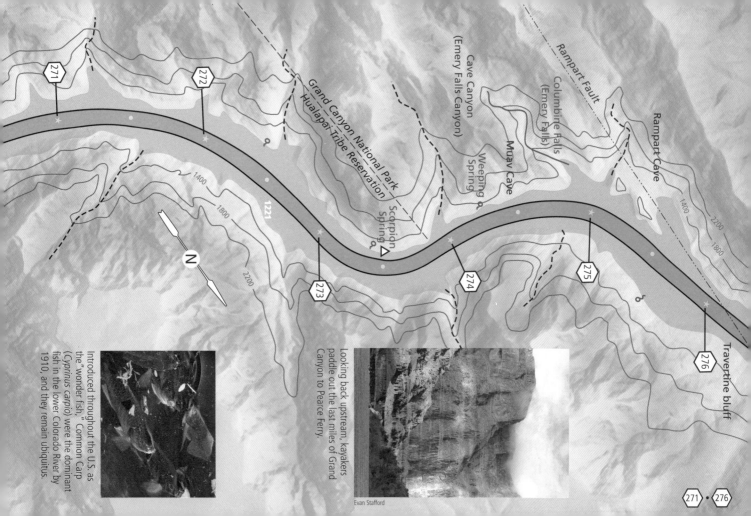

271

272

Grand Canyon National Park
Hualapai Tribe Reservation

Cave Canyon
(Emery Falls Canyon)

Rampart Fault

Columbine Falls
(Emery Falls)

Rampart Cave

Mnav Cave

Weeping
Spring

1400

1800

1221

Scorpion
Spring

N

2200

273

274

275

276

Travertine bluff

1400

2200

1800

Introduced throughout the U.S. as
the "wonder fish," Common Carp
(Cyprinus carpio) were the dominant
fish in the lower Colorado River by
1910, and they remain ubiquitous.

Looking back upstream, kayakers
paddle out the last miles of Grand
Canyon to Pearce Ferry.

Evan Stafford

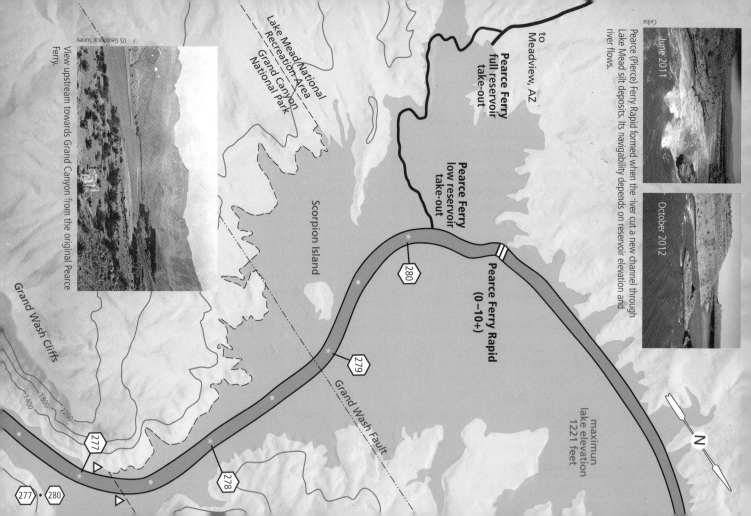

Pearce (Pierce) Ferry Rapid formed when the river cut a new channel through Lake Mead silt deposits. Its navigability depends on reservoir elevation and river flows.

June 2011

October 2012

Ceiba

to Meadview, AZ

Pearce Ferry full reservoir take-out

Pearce Ferry low reservoir take-out

Pearce Ferry Rapid (0–10+)

Scorpion Island

Grand Wash Fault

maximum lake elevation 1221 feet

Lake Mead National Recreation Area

Grand Canyon National Park

Grand Wash Cliffs

1400
1800
2200

280

279

278

277

N

View upstream towards Grand Canyon from the original Pearce Ferry.

US Geological Survey

277 • 280

II. GEOGRAPHY: WHERE ARE WE?

The Colorado River and the Colorado Plateau

The Colorado River is the primary river of the American Southwest, providing water and energy to nearly 40 million people from Texas to Los Angeles, and north to Wyoming. The 7th largest river in the coterminous United States, it is 1,450 mi (2,333 km) long and drains 246,000 sq mi (637,137 km^2) through parts of seven US and two Mexican states, and through two geologic provinces. The southern half, from the river's mouth at the head of the Sea of Cortez upstream to Grand Wash in upper Lake Mead, lies in the Basin and Range geologic province. The northern half of the drainage, including Grand Canyon, lies in the Colorado Plateau geologic province (Fig. 2.1). The Colorado Plateau covers more than 157,000 mi^2 (406,454 km^2) of Wyoming, Colorado, Utah, New Mexico, and Arizona. It includes the river basins of the Colorado, Green, Gunnison, White, San Juan, Little Colorado, and Virgin Rivers, as well as wide plateaus, spires, buttes, and high mountains, long ridges and scarps, and innumerable lesser drainages.

The Colorado River emerges at 10,184 ft (3,104 m) in a springfed marsh lake in La Poudre Pass in Rocky Mountain National Park, and in the Green River basin at Gannet Peak in the Wind River Range at 13,804 ft (4,207 m). Upstream from Grand Canyon, the Green and Colorado Rivers and their tributaries carve spectacular canyons, including the Black Canyon of the Gunnison, Split Mountain, Lodore, Stillwater, Dolores, Cataract, and Glen Canyons, each renown for its stunning scenery and extraordinary river running.

In northern Arizona, more than half of the distance down its course and the start of our river journey, the Colorado River reaches the Kaibab Limestone at the mouth

"This is nothing like Grand Cayman."

(statement by a disgruntled passenger to her husband while stepping off a motor rig at the mouth of the Little Colorado River)

"On the 28th (of March 1826), we reached a point of the river where the mountains shut in so close upon its shores, that we were compelled to...travel along the acclivity, the river still in sight, and at an immense depth beneath us... A march more gloomy and heart-wearing, to people hungry, poorly clad, and mourning the loss of their companions, cannot be imagined. April 10th, we arrived where the river emerges from these horrid mountains... No mortal has the power of describing the pleasure I felt, when I could once more reach the banks of the river."

James Ohio Pattie[137, 137a]

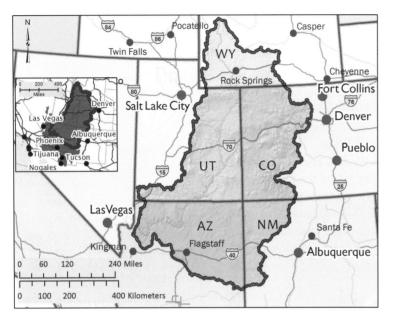

Figure 2.1
Colorado Plateau and inset of Colorado River drainage area.

of the Paria River, and enters Grand Canyon. Grand Canyon is 277 miles (446 km) long, with distances traditionally measured from Lees Ferry (Mile 0), and the side of the river is designated as left or right, looking downstream (Fig. 2.2). The Canyon's rock layers are rather steeply inclined to the south between Lees Ferry and the Upper Granite Gorge near Phantom Ranch at Mile 88. The river cuts into the Kaibab Plateau, rather than flowing around it, exposing dozens of colorful, neatly stacked, Proterozoic and Paleozoic strata. On the north side of the river, the Kaibab Plateau is uplifted, elevating that low, broad dome nearly 2,000 ft (600 m) higher than the South Rim. Further downstream, these strata partially descend back into the Earth's surface, creating a rolling terrain. All of this canyon country is deeply dissected by innumerable tributary canyons.

The dramatic rims of Grand Canyon encompass an area of 1.67 million ac (6,758 km²) on the southern Colorado Plateau. Of this, 925,000 ac (3,743 km²; about 55%) lie within Grand Canyon National Park, with the rest on the Havasupai, Hualapai and Navajo Reservations, and with small areas on Lake Mead and Glen Canyon National Recreation Areas, Kaibab National Forest, the Bureau of Land Management's Arizona Strip District, and with Arizona State land in the Little Colorado River and upper Kanab and Havasu (Cataract) drainages. Land area is traditionally measured in planview (2 dimensions), which works well in Kansas, but the surface area of Grand Canyon increases by more than 23% to 2.06 million ac (8,322 km²) when measured in three dimensions, with its many cliff faces. The volume of Grand Canyon is about 720 mi³ (3,000 km³), depending on which surface area interpolation technique is used.

Glen Canyon Dam lies 15.8 mi (25 km) upstream from Lees Ferry. Between the dam and Separation Canyon (Mile 240, Rkm 386) on uppermost Lake Mead, the Colorado

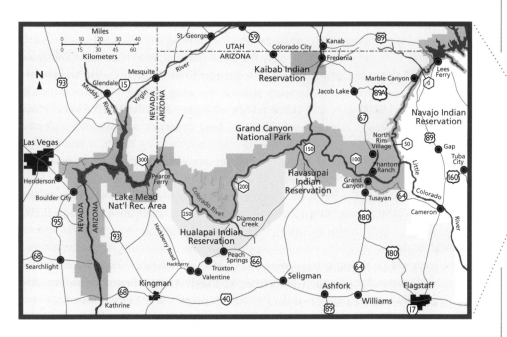

Figure 2.2
Grand Canyon Region

River flows uninterrupted for 255 mi (411 km). Its average depth is about 33 ft (10 m), and reaches a maximum depth of about 90 ft (27.5 m) near Boulder Narrows (Mile 19) and Granite Narrows (Mile 135). Above Diamond Creek, the river varies in width from 76 ft (23.1 m) at Mile 135 to more than 600 ft (182 m) in the wider reaches, and drops at an average gradient of about 8 ft/mi (1.5 m/km). The river falls a total of 1,900 ft (580 m) between Lees Ferry and Lake Mead. Half of the river's drop takes place in the more than 165 rapids, but rapids account for only 9% of the total distance through the Canyon. The more than 600 tributaries of the Colorado River in Grand Canyon[112] typically occur on or near faults or fractures.

The South Rim generally drains away from the Canyon, and south-side tributaries are generally short, except for the Little Colorado River, Havasu Creek, and drainages from Diamond Creek to the west. Surface flow is towards the Canyon from the North Rim, and north-side tributaries are often longer, particularly in the lower Canyon. Longer drainages can convey flash floods long distances, making hiking a risky undertaking during the summer monsoons.

Near the head of Lake Mead the Colorado River crosses the Grand Wash Fault. There, at the boundary between the Colorado Plateau geologic province and the vast, unruly, extensional terrain of the Basin and Range province, the orderly strata exposed by the river are downthrown more than 2 miles (3.35 km) and Grand Canyon abruptly ends.

Spatial Scale

The complete picture of the geography of Grand Canyon takes shape across spatial scale. In northern Arizona, the Colorado River snakes its way through broad, mostly flat tablelands. At this regional scale, Grand Canyon consists of two basins: an isolated eastern basin that receives the flows of the Paria and Little Colorado River (LCR) drainages, and a more open western basin that connects western Grand Canyon to the Mohave and Sonoran deserts to the west and south (Fig. 2.3).[19] The two basins are separated by the steep, narrow 35 km-long Muav Gorge, which creates a formidable, cliff-dominated barrier to upstream and downstream dispersal of numerous southwestern plants, invertebrates, and vertebrates.[113, 270]

Within the Colorado River corridor, and as a result of Glen Canyon Dam, the mainstream exists in three turbidity (water clarity) segments: the clearwater segment from Glen Canyon Dam to the mouth of the Paria River, the variably turbid (silty) segment between the Paria and LCR, and the usually turbid segment downstream from the LCR confluence.[281] These segments are steps in the recovery of the river from the impacts of Glen Canyon Dam. As the river flows downstream from the dam water temperature, geochemistry, and sediment contributed by tributaries produces conditions in the river approaching those of pre-dam time when the river was far more sediment-laden and seasonally warm.[135]

At a finer scale, within turbidity segments, the river corridor consists of 13 geo-

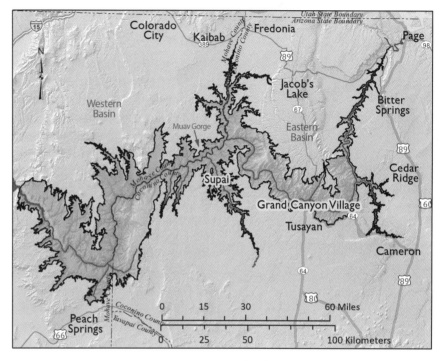

Figure 2.3
The rim map of Grand Canyon.[19]

Table 2.1. Geomorphic Reaches

Segment	Name	Reach Endpoints (mi, km)	Mean Width (m)
1. CW	Glen Canyon	-15.3–0.7 (-25.0–1.0)	188
2. VT	Permian Gorge	0.7–11 (1.0–17.7)	85
3. VT	Supai Gorge	11–23 (17.7–37)	64
4. VT	Redwall Gorge	23–39 (37–62.7)	67
5. VT	Marble Canyon	39–61.5 (62.7–98.9)	107
6. UT	Furnace Flats	61.5–77 (98.9–124)	119
7. UT	Upper Granite Gorge	77–119.5 (124–192.3)	58
8. UT	The Aisles	119.5–127 (192.3–204.3)	70
9. UT	Middle Granite Gorge	127–140.5 (204.3–226.1)	64
10. UT	Muav Gorge	140.5–160.5 (226.1–258.2)	55
11. UT	Lower Canyon Reach	160.5–214.5 (258.2–345.2)	94
12. UT	Lower Granite Gorge	214.5–240 (345.2–386.2)	73
13. UT	Upper Lake Mead	240–279 (386.2–449)	235

The bedrock- and landform-defined geomorphic reaches of the Colorado River in Grand Canyon. Distance is measured from the U.S. Geological Survey Lees Ferry streamflow gauge, which lies 15.8 mi (25 km) downstream from Glen Canyon Dam. Turbidity segments include the clearwater (CW), variably turbid (VT), and usually turbid (UT) segments. Reach names were modified.[279] Reach width (m) was measured at a mainstream flow of 24,000 cfs (680 m³/s) for reaches 1–12, and a Lake Mead pool surface elevation of 1,200 ft (365 m).[244, 279]

morphic reaches prescribed by the bedrock through which the river runs (Table 2.1).[244, 281] These reaches generally vary by width and depth, as well as average flow velocity, the severity of their rapids, the number and size of eddies, cover of riparian vegetation, density of beavers, campsite availability, and access to tributaries and the rim. The river is wider and shallower, and contains more, larger eddies in reaches where it cuts through shales, including the Permian, Marble Canyon, and Furnace Flats Reaches. The obvious exception is the Lower Canyon Reach, which is relatively wide, but contains Lava Falls Rapid. In contrast, the mainstream is narrower and contains more large, severe rapids in reaches dominated by limestone and metamorphic rocks (e.g., the Supai and Redwall Gorges, and the Granite Gorges, respectively). The strata into which the Canyon descends tilt up to the south from Lees Ferry to Phantom Ranch, then tilt more-or-less downward from Phantom to the middle of Grand Canyon, and thereafter gently roll downstream to the Hurricane Fault below Whitmore Rapid. In the first 180 miles of its course, the suite of bedrock-defined geomorphic reaches is a partial mirror image of itself, at least from the standpoint of stratigraphy, geomorphology, and ecology, if not archeology and our experience of the Canyon.

Zooming in further, to the scale of individual rapids, the Colorado River channel is generally V- or broadly U-shaped, with associated terraces along the channel margins.

However, the uniformity of the channel is regularly interrupted by debris fans at the mouths of the many tributaries that reach the mainstream in Grand Canyon (Fig. 2.4). Fan-eddy complexes constrict the river to form riffles or rapids, which are relatively shallow, but sit atop a deep plunge pool, with the floor of the river fanning out and shallowing downstream as the river leaves the constriction of the rapids. The river then returns to its normal, relatively uniform channel shape within that reach. These debris fans are fixed features that create recirculation zones and during descending flows, deposit sand in characteristic locations both upstream and downstream of the

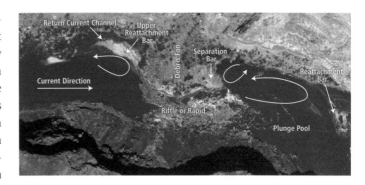

Figure 2.4
The debris fan-eddy complex at RM 43.5

constriction. Therefore, unlike rivers that flow unconstrained across a flood plain, such as the Mississippi, the locations of sandbars along the Colorado River remain fixed.

Fan-eddy complexes generate a distinctive suite of riparian habitats, each with discrete grain sizes, soils, stage-elevation relationships, inundation frequencies, and riparian vegetation in zones according to height above the river.[47, 244, 279] A submerged or subaerial upper pool sandbar commonly forms upstream from a rapid, which also often contains a return current channel as well as associated riparian terraces (Fig. 2.4). The debris fan itself often displays stage-stratified terraces and riparian vegetation. Downstream from the debris dam, two types of sandbars develop: 1) a separation sandbar at the base of the debris fan, often with a counter eddy if the eddy system is sufficiently large; and 2) a reattachment sandbar at the point where the current reattaches to shore. Downstream reattachment bars also commonly support stage-stratified terraces and a return current channel. The 13 geomorphic reaches of the river vary in the abundance of fan-eddy complexes, and whether and how long they retain sand, with narrow reaches having fewer

Elevation

Elevation in the Grand Canyon region strongly affects microclimate, plant and animal community composition and distribution, and microsite ecology.[270] Following the ideas of Alexander Von Humboldt,[316] C.H. Merriam was the first American naturalist to relate biological zonation to elevation, using a transect from the floor of Grand Canyon to the 12,633 ft (3,851 m) top of the San Francisco Peaks outside of Flagstaff, and into the nearby Sonoran and Painted Deserts.[202] Merriam attributed the discrete zonation of trees across elevation in the Grand Canyon region primarily to temperature and latitude; however, Holdridge[134] and others subsequently recognized the importance of seasonal and total precipitation, evapotranspiration, soil, and the other factors controlling vegetation and development of natural communities.

Elevation lowers air temperature and freeze-thaw cycle frequency, and increases precipitation and relative humidity. Globally, ascending in elevation lowers the temperature 3°F/1000 ft (6.5 °C/km). However, comparison of air temperatures at Phantom Ranch with the South Rim from 1941-2003 shows a rate of change of -4.8°F/1000 ft (-7.4°C/km). This rate of change is more than 1.3-fold steeper than the norm, probably because of the dark rock colors in the inner canyon and aspect, the cardinal direction that the canyon walls face.

sand bars and more rapid erosion, and wide reaches having more sandbars. The suite of habitats at debris fans provides the template for vegetation and wildlife habitat development, as well as archeological and river campsites. The mainstream ecosystem is remarkable in supporting such a great abundance of ecologically replicated eddy-fan habitats.

Weather

The climate of the Colorado River corridor is continental and arid, variable and often harsh. As the river descends in elevation from 3,116 ft (950 m) at Lees Ferry to about 1,200 ft (370 m) on Lake Mead, the mean annual temperature rises from 63°F to 66°F (17°C to 19°C), but the monthly mean temperature is highest at Phantom Ranch (Fig. 2.5). Daily minimum and maximum temperatures commonly fluctuate 20–30°F (11–17°C), are seasonal, and are strongly controlled by elevation.

Total annual precipitation averages 6.6 in at Lees Ferry, 9.6 in (244 mm) at Phantom Ranch (2,400 ft, 732 m; from 1976–2012), and about 3.5 in (89 mm) on Lake Mead (Fig. 2.6). Precipitation varies across elevation, commonly with 50-100% greater precipitation on the South Rim (6,800 ft, 2,073 m elevation) and 50-300% more on the North Rim (8,500 ft, 2,591 m), as compared to that at Phantom Ranch. Precipitation is highly variable year to year, ranging from 3–15 in (76–380 mm) annually at Phantom Ranch. A large portion of this annual precipitation falls during the summer "monsoon" or rainy season between mid-July and early October. Precipitation is greatest every five to seven years during "El Nino" Southern (Pacific) Oscillation events.

The Seasons

The following descriptions of the seasons are based on weather data collected at Phantom Ranch since 1931 and more recently in the river corridor.[73, 252]

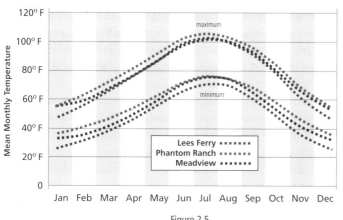

Figure 2.5

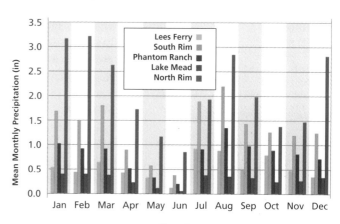

Figure 2.6

Spring (March 22 to June 21) follows a gradual but irregular warming trend as the frequency of moisture-laden Pacific storms decreases. The clear spells may be ridiculously windy. Average high temperatures range from 82°F (28°C) in April to 101°F (38°C) in June, and daily low temperatures range from 56°F (13°C) to 72°F (22°C) for the same period. Variable and unseasonable weather is to be expected in spring. June is often relentlessly clear and hot.

Summer (June 22 to September 21) is hot, particularly in July, when the average daily highs exceed 106°F (41°C). Air temperatures in excess of 121°F (49°C) at Mile 220 were reported in June of 1990 and soil surface temperatures sometimes exceed 170°F (77°C). The summer rainy season usually begins in mid-July, bringing much-needed rain and cloudy afternoons. Low pressure aloft and intense solar heating of the Canyon

Figure 2.5

Monthly average air temperature (in): Phantom Ranch has generally higher average air temperatures than either Lees Ferry or Meadview.[252, NOAA]

Figure 2.6

Monthly average precipitation: All stations report a distinctive mid- to late-summer increase in precipitation during the summer monsoons.[252, NOAA]

floor and walls can cause strong but local thermal uplifting. Moist oceanic air is drawn up and condensed into thunderheads which, by mid-afternoon, release rain and hail at rates of up to several inches per hour. Local flooding and rock fall often occur at this time. We have a saying in the Southwest that "It doesn't rain often here, but you better watch out the day it does." One day in August, 1951, a single thunderstorm dropped 2.7 in (69 mm) of rain at Phantom Ranch! *Virga* (rain that evaporates before reaching the ground) and magnificent rainbows are frequently associated with these summer monsoons. Rains subside and the sky generally clears in the evening, but even during the heat of summer these storms can produce chilly weather.

Fall (September 22 to December 21) becomes progressively cooler and drier. Average daily highs range from 85°F (29°C) in October to 57°F (14°C) in December, and average daily lows vary from 59°F (15°C) to 37°F (3°C) over the same period. November and December become increasingly subject to low-pressure disturbances and Pacific winter storms.

Winter (December 22 to March 21) weather is unstable, with several possible storm tracks (southwestern, western, or northern). These storms frequently bring rain or snow. Almost 11 in (28 mm) of snow fell in one day at Phantom Ranch in February, 1939, and some snow falls at Phantom Ranch nearly every year. It is not unusual for riverside sandbars to freeze in winter, for ice to form along the margins of the river, and for boat frames to ice up and become dangerously slippery. Winter temperatures range from an average daily high of 56°F (13°C) in January to 70°F (21°C) in March. The average daily lows vary from 36°F to 47°F (2-8°C) between January and March. Overall, it is best to be prepared for unexpected weather in Grand Canyon.

Out here, it's so hot that.....

The "W" Word

Wind during the daylight hours usually blows upstream in Grand Canyon. Rising hot air from the Canyon floor also causes diurnal upstream air movement and hot, dry mountain-valley winds that can blow fiercely. Arizona's prevailing winds are southwesterly, and those sections of the Canyon that run westward or southward catch this wind face-first. However, sections of the Canyon that flow to the north or northeast (i.e., the Deubendorff to Tapeats Creek stretch, and some places below Diamond Creek) sustain downstream winds during the day. Normally, the only other times that strong, downstream winds occur is just before downpours. The general pattern of swirling wind around tributary mouths is intriguing, but so far remains unstudied.

At night, cool air subsides from the rims and in summer creates a light, distinctive downstream breeze. Smoke from forest fires on the rims usually rather abruptly ceases rising at sunset, and falls into the Canyon, sometimes making for smokey mornings on the river. In winter, cold air subsidence can bring brutally cold conditions for river runners. A hard freeze in December 1990 killed much of the hot-desert brittlebush (*Encelia farinosa*) in upper Marble Canyon. Winter cold air subsidence is a primary reason that large succulent cacti like saguaro cannot survive on the floor of Grand Canyon.

Climate Change

Climate change predictions for northern Arizona indicate increased variability along with extremes of temperature and storm frequency, and no models predict increased precipitation. The Bureau of Reclamation[300] conducted a 50-yr modeling analysis of climate change and changing water and hydroelectric power demand impacts on the Colorado River Basin water and power production. This exhaustive analysis considered four sets of climate models against six variables, which were related to the performance of

Aspect

Aspect strongly affects many facets of Canyon ecology. Steep south-facing slopes, especially with darker rock colors, absorb and re-radiate more heat than north-facing slopes, which often are shaded from direct sunlight, and are cooler and more humid across elevation. The Canyon walls that do receive and trap solar radiation release heat slowly, keeping relative humidity extremely low. One consequence of elevated mean annual temperatures is that dry Grand Canyon caves are generally too warm in winter for bat hibernation. In contrast to the broad effects of elevation, aspect exerts strong control locally over microclimate and potential evapotranspiration and productivity.

Sunlight is the driver for most of the terrestrial realm, but the tall, steep cliffs of Grand Canyon make it a sunlight-limited ecosystem.[270, 339] North-facing slopes in east-west flowing river segments in the deepest portions of the Canyon receive the least sunlight. Overall, the percent of potential sunlight received on the floor of Grand Canyon is about 70% of that available on the rims. Reaches differ: the steep, narrow, west-flowing Muav Gorge receives 55% of ambient sunlight, and almost no direct sun in winter. In contrast, the relatively wide Permian, Furnace Flats, and Lower Granite Gorge reaches receive 75–88% of ambient solar radiation.

Humidity

As in all desert areas, evaporation substantially exceeds precipitation in the Grand Canyon region. More than 90% of the in-coming precipitation simply evaporates, and more than seven vertical feet of water are lost to evaporation from the surfaces of Lakes Powell and Mead every year,[37] compared to the 3.5 inches (8.9 mm) of precipitation that fall there annually. Low humidity and high summertime temperatures mean that Grand Canyon vegetation becomes increasingly leafless at lower elevations. The only places where desert plants can afford large leaves are along waterways, or in the shadiest of nooks on north-facing slopes.

Cold water temperatures along the river strongly affect riparian climate. A belt of humid air lies on the river surface. This boundary layer decreases to less than one foot (35 cm) during hot summer days, but commonly expands at night up to 7-10 ft (2-3 m) above the river.[263] Sound travels better in humid air, so leaning over the river at night, one often can hear water noises, like nearby rapids, more clearly. Rarely, early morning fog develops on the river, showing how that belt of humid air moves and responds to wind and sunlight.

the Bureau's Colorado River water and power delivery system. River resource categories included water delivery, electrical power production, water quality, flood control, recreational and ecological resources. The Bureau concluded that the water and energy supply system was likely to be vulnerable 2–3% of the time at Lees Ferry from 2041–2060, but was likely to be vulnerable 19% of that time at Hoover Dam. Thus the Upper Basin's river "goods and services" may be slightly negatively affected by climate change, whereas those of the Lower Basin are likely to be substantially affected. A more bleak perspective suggests that global conditions are so altered by human impacts that future changes in climate and water supplies may be outside the bounds of past scenarios. By this view, our future weather has never been less certain.[207]

III. GEOLOGIC HISTORY OF GRAND CANYON (In Memoriam: William J. Breed 1928–2013)

Overview [15b,17, 28, 54, 72, 177, 293]

At a total depth of 1.54 mi (2.48 km) from the North Rim down to Lake Mead, Grand Canyon is not the deepest canyon on Earth. That record belongs to the 2.08 mi (3.35 km)-deep Cotahuasi Canyon in southwestern Peru. Nor is Grand Canyon the longest canyon—the Indus and Ganges Rivers have far longer submarine canyons, extending southward across the floor of the Indian Ocean. Nor does Grand Canyon contain the world's oldest rock: Canada, Australia, South Africa and Greenland all have older strata. The basement rocks of Laurentia, the original North American craton (continent) extend back more than 2.5 billion years (b.y.) ago, and the Acasta Gneiss in the Canadian Shield and the Nuvvuagittua greenstone belt around Hudson Bay date to between 4.04-4.38 b.y.[26a, 220a] What sets Grand Canyon apart from all other landscapes on Earth is its extraordinarily intact geologic history—its strata dating back more than 1.8 b.y., with many intervening periods of geologic history represented in its cliffs and slopes. Nearly every natural environment one can imagine has existed at one time or another at the place we now call Grand Canyon: deserts, mountains, shallow and deep seas, swamps, and rivers—many of which left geologic clues of their existence—are stacked here in sequence, showing us the magnificent dynamism of our Earth. In this chapter we explore that geologic history, what can be known about the formation of Grand Canyon, and how the Colorado River functions as a geomorphic agent.

But before beginning up those trails there are a few geological concepts and processes that may help us see the landscapes around us in a more integrated fashion. We will first discuss geologic time, some basic rules of geology, a few definitions, and background information before delving into the extraordinary chronology and history of the strata that make up this portion of the Earth's crust.

A Few Geological Definitions and Concepts

Completeness of the Geologic Record: Despite the exposure of more than 1.8 b.y. of the Earth's history in two dozen strata in Grand Canyon, the rocks do not represent continuous deposition over time: much more geologic time is missing from the stack of sediments than is present. So numerous are the unconformities among the strata that although John Wesley Powell considered the geology of the Canyon to be an open book that "…I can read as I run…",[230] the book is actually missing most of its pages. The Great Unconformity involves up to 1.2 b.y. of no or missing deposition, and several other unconformities each lasted more than 100 m.y.[151]

Erosion: Even a quick glance at Grand Canyon's walls reveals a structured series of sheer cliffs and talus slopes (eroded loose rock) that are the result of differential erosion of various bedrock types. Buried strata withstand the vertical pressure imposed by overlying formations, but once strata are exposed at the surface they erode at very different rates. Shales, siltstones, and soft sandstones, such as the Hermit and Bright Angel Shales and the Dox Formation, are easily weathered and undercut, causing the overlying layers to collapse. As soft strata erode back they leave broad, low-angle talus slopes that serve as the foundations for overlying harder, less erodible strata. Sandstone, limestone, and dolomite (limestone containing magnesium) are more resistant to erosion, as the Coconino and Tapeats Sandstones and the Redwall Limestone demonstrate by forming vertical cliffs. Even more resistant are igneous rocks, such as basalt (lava), the chemically similar rock diabase, and granite. Hardest but most brittle are crystalline metamorphic rocks, such as the schists and gneisses of the Inner Gorge. The river's rate of downcutting through these different rock types has varied considerably. But while the river has been responsible for downcutting and is the conduit for sediment transport, lateral erosion from freezing and thawing, and the action of tributary sidestreams, has produced a canyon that is 17 miles (27 km) wide in western Grand Canyon, but only 3000 feet deep.

Unconformities: An *unconformity* is a contact between strata that marks an erosional interval or an interruption in deposition. Several kinds of unconformities occur. 1) A *nonconformity* is deposition on igneous or metamorphic strata (e.g., the contact of the Tapeats Formation on top of Vishnu Schist). 2) An *angular unconformity* involves deposition of sedimentary rock on top of folded and tilted strata (e.g., the base of the Cambrian strata on top of the Grand Canyon Supergroup). 3) A *disconformity* is an erosional plane within flat-lying sedimentary rocks that marks a period of erosion or non-deposition. Many Paleozoic formations in Grand Canyon are separated by disconformities. A minor disconformity is called a *diastem*. 4) A *paraconformity* is an undetectable break in deposition or a cryptic erosional plane that may only be detectable as an unconformity in the fossil assemblage. Thus, the "Great Unconformity" noted by Powell and named by Dutton in 1882,[74] consists of both nonconformities and angular unconformities.[151]

Geologic Formations: A geologic formation consists of one or more rock strata that develop over a discrete time interval in a more-or-less consistent environment. A geologic formation may consist of any one of the three rock types (igneous, sedimentary, or metamorphic rocks), and formations are named for the nearest named locality. Hence, the Tapeats Formation (the Tapeats Sandstone) was named by L.F. Nobel[216] through his studies in Tapeats Creek in central Grand Canyon. Formations are subdivided into members. The base of a formation is often marked by a basal conglomerate, such as the Hotauta Conglomerate at the base of the Bass Formation. A suite of formations is called a group, such as the Tonto Group (the Tapeats to Muav formations), and a larger assemblage of formations may be called a supergroup (e.g., the Precambrian sedimentary and igneous Grand Canyon Supergroup), when the formations collectively encompass a period of environmental consistency.

Geochronology: A Brief History of Earth (Table 3.1)

Earth is 4.57 b.y. old, probably having formed through condensation and runaway accretion of gas and materials around a solar nebula that became our sun well after the Big Bang (13.8 b.y. ago). The first stage of the Earth's history is called the **Hadean Eon** (4.57 to 3.8 b.y. ago). During the Hadean, Earth was subject to giant meteorite impacts, including a collision with a protoplanet the size of Mars that blasted a mass of the Earth's crust into orbit, creating our moon. Earth underwent the Late Heavy Bombardment from 4.1-3.8 b.y. ago, during which time multiple, massive meteorite strikes occurred, perhaps repeatedly vaporizing the entire crust. During the Hadean, massive, global volcanism occurred, and the oceans formed, with much water contributed through comet collisions as well as earth degassing. Life may have arisen or arrived on Earth during the Hadean Eon or shortly thereafter biogenesis may have occurred at or near seafloor volcanic vents where sufficient methane, ammonium, and free phosphate might have been available for development of early ribozymes, precursors to RNA.[317]

During the **Archean Eon** (3.8–2.5 b.y. ago) the early sun was fainter and the Earth was hotter, making tectonic subduction at plate margins more rapid. Consequently, early continents (cratons) were smaller, growing gradually by accretion of sea-floor materials and/or deposition of early continental crustal materials. Single-celled life, including cyanobacteria (single-celled, photosynthetic blue-green algae), was abundant but anaerobic, existing in an atmosphere mostly derived from volcanism and rich in carbon dioxide, methane, and sulfur, and therefore inhospitable to life forms requiring free atmospheric oxygen.[158]

The beginning of the **Proterozoic Eon** (2.5-0.54 b.y. ago) saw many geological developments. Cyanobacteria had been releasing free oxygen (O^2) as a waste product, a process that culminated in Proterozoic time with the "Oxygen Catastrophe," transitioning the Earth's atmosphere from an anoxic state to one dominated by free oxygen. This and subsequent oxygenation may be related to the Huronian (2.4–2.1 b.y. ago) and subsequent Precambrian glaciation events, which may have created a "Snowball Earth,"[162a] as well as precipitation of iron oxide throughout the world. Much of the iron we use today is derived from these early Proterozoic "banded iron" deposits.

Geologic Time

Geologic time has been a primary focus of research for 250 years, and with modern methods, our understanding of time has grown enormously.[319] Many thousands of human lives and millions of person-hours of critical thought and testing have produced a profound scientific understanding of Earth's history. Science is a rigorous debate about the nature of the material world. As with theories of gravity, plate tectonics, and evolution, much of the debate about the geologic chronology of the planet has been resolved, but not all mysteries have been solved—in fact, there is more to wonder about than ever. Nonetheless, tremendous scientific effort has produced extraordinary insights into Earth's past, including the wanderings of our peregrine continents. But as for geologic time, it is simply impossible for humans to intuitively grasp its vastness. While we continue to wonder at the magnitude of time, it is easier to simply consider geologic time as an organizational framework or a roadmap, rather than as an intuitive phenomenon.[51, 105, 319] Figs. 3.1 and 3.2 lay out Earth's roadmap of time and history.

EON	ERA	PERIOD	EPOCH	START m.y.ago	EVENTS
PHANEROZOIC	CENOZOIC	NEOGENE	HOLOCENE	0.1	Human history
			PLEISTOCENE	2.6	Ice ages
			PLIOCENE	5.9	Ancestral humans
			MIOCENE	23	Basin & Range orogeny
		PALEOGENE	OLIGOCENE	33.9	Modern climate
			EOCENE	56	Thermal maximum
			PALEOCENE	66	Rise of mammals
	MESOZOIC	CRETACEOUS		145	Primates
		JURASSIC		201	Birds Flowering Plants
		TRIASSIC		252	Dinosaurs Mammals
	PALEOZOIC	PERMIAN		299	Pangaea
		PENSYLVANIAN CARBONIFEROUS MISSISSIPPIAN		323	Conifers Reptiles
				359	Proto-dragonflies
		DEVONIAN		419	Ferns Amphibians
		SILURIAN		444	Land Plants
		ORDOVICIAN		485	Insects / Fish
		CAMBRIAN		541	Trilobites
CRYPTOZOIC	PROTEROZOIC	NEOPROTEROZOIC		1000	Ediacara, First Animals
		MESOPROTEROZOIC		1600	
		PALEOPROTEROZOIC		2500	
	ARCHEAN	The Precambrian Eons account for 88% of the earth's history.		4000	Blue-green Algae Bacteria Oldest Rocks Oldest fossil life
	HADEAN			4570	Earth & Moon form

Table 3.1
The Geologic Time Scale [51, 105, 319]

Development of the Earth's Crust

Three thick groups of rock strata are exposed in Grand Canyon, the oldest of which dates back nearly 2 b.y., or about 40% of the Earth's history. Each package of rock represents a revolution of the "rock cycle," the continuous process through which the strata that make up the Earth's crust are deposited, lithified, and then eroded away, with the eroded material contributing to future rock formation. Each of these three rock cycles has taken about half a billion years. The first (deepest) group of rocks exposed in Grand Canyon involved transformation of sedimentary and igneous rock into metamorphic basement rock, from about 2.0-1.6 b.y. ago.[156] Oldest within these rocks is the Elves Chasm Gneiss, a granite that crystallized 1.84 b.y. ago. The **Vishnu Schist** was deposited as a set of submarine sedimentary deposits about 1.75 b.y. ago. Mineral grains in these sediments date back 3.3 b.y., indicating that older crust was recycled into early depositional basins. Magma repeatedly intruded into the metamorphosing Vishnu Schist, and is visible today as veins of ingeous granite. The Vishnu Schist formed the roots of an ancient mountain belt (the Vishnu Mountains) from 1.75-1.66 b.y. ago.

The second package of rocks involved deposition of 14,000 ft (4.3 km) of Precambrian sedimentary and igneous rock in the **Grand Canyon Supergroup** between 1.25 b.y. ago and 742 million years (m.y.) ago. These rocks were deposited after the Vishnu Mountains had been eroded down to a flat, seafloor plane. After 742 m.y. ago another period of uplift, tilting, and erosion occurred, preserving remnants of the Supergroup only in a series of buried fault wedges in the Grand Canyon region.[78, 294]

The third group of rocks resulted from Phanerozoic (visible life) Eon deposition of Grand Canyon's **Paleozoic Era** strata, beginning 541 m.y. ago. Some of these rock layers contain abundant fossils. Mesozoic strata, some containing dinosaur fossils were deposited across the region 251-66 m.y. ago. Some Mesozoic strata are still visible near Lees Ferry, most have been eroded from much of the region. The Grand Canyon region was lifted above sea level beginning in the Triassic Period, changing the region from a depositional to a primarily erosional landscape. Thus, each of the three goups of rocks involved deposition, lithification, uplift, and subsequent erosion of thick beds of rock over about half a billion years. We are eroding our way through the third rock cycle.

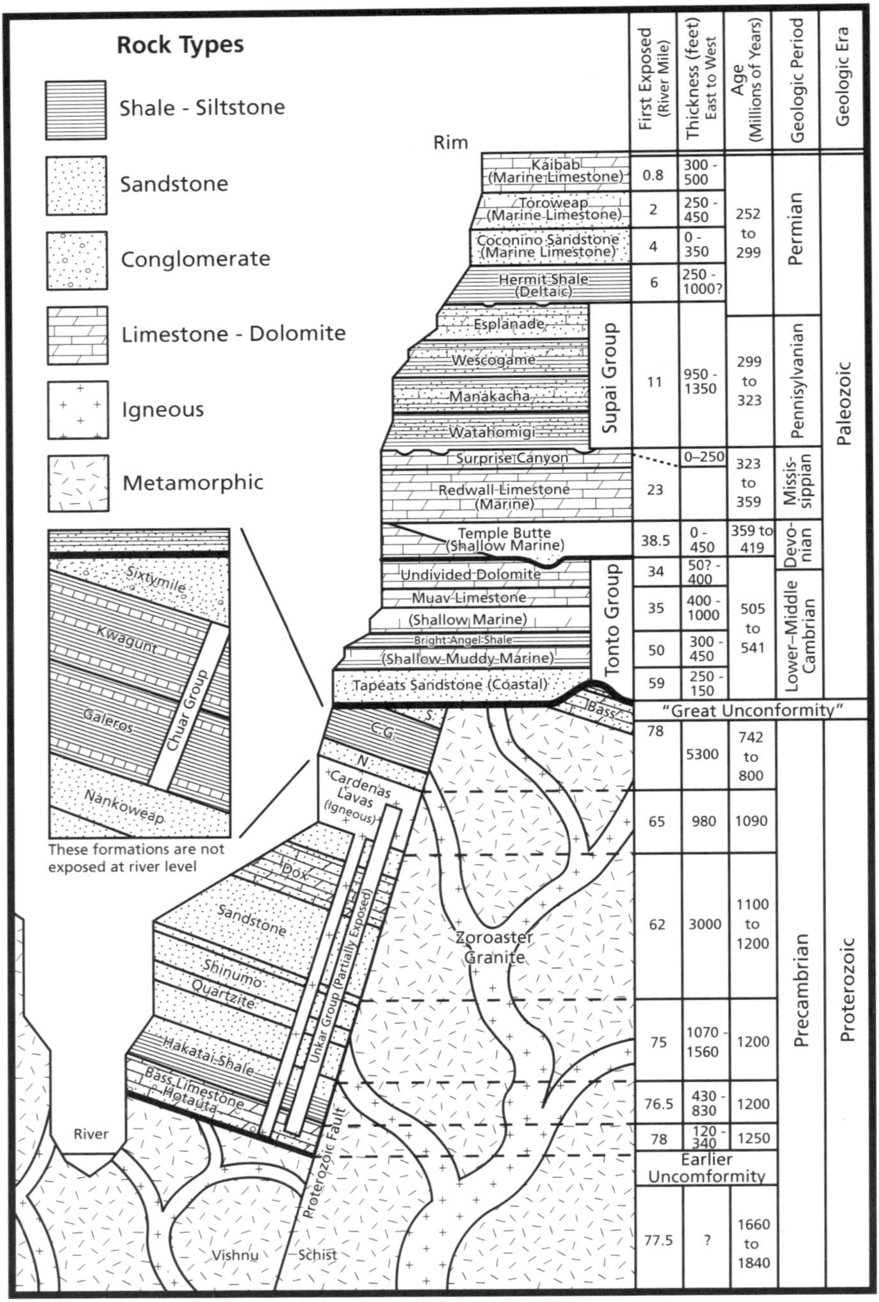

Figure 3.1 — Stratigraphy of Grand Canyon region

Geologic Era	Paleozoic									Proterozoic					
Geologic Period	Permian				Pennsylvanian	Missis-sippian	Devo-nian	Lower-Middle Cambrian			Precambrian					
Age (Millions of Years)	252 to 299				299 to 323	323 to 359	359 to 419	505 to 541			742 to 800	1090	1100 to 1200	1200	1250	1660 to 1840
Thickness (feet) East to West	300-500	250-450	0-350	250-1000?	950-1350	0-250	0-450	507-400	400-1000	300-450 / 250-150	5300	980	3000	1070-1560	430-830 / 120-340	?
First Exposed (River Mile)	0.8	2	4	6	11	23	38.5	34	35	50 / 59	78	65	62	75	76.5 / 78	77.5

"Great Unconformity" — Earlier Unconformity

Supai Group — **Tonto Group**

Formations (Rim, East to West):
- Kaibab (Marine Limestone)
- Toroweap (Marine Limestone)
- Coconino Sandstone (Marine Limestone)
- Hermit Shale (Deltaic)
- Esplanade
- Wescogame
- Manakacha
- Watahomigi
- Surprise Canyon
- Redwall Limestone (Marine)
- Temple Butte (Shallow Marine)
- Undivided Dolomite
- Muav Limestone (Shallow Marine)
- Bright Angel Shale (Shallow-Muddy-Marine)
- Tapeats Sandstone (Coastal)

Proterozoic units: Cardenas Lavas (Igneous), Dox Sandstone, Shinumo Quartzite, Hakatai Shale, Bass Limestone, Hotauta; Unkar Group (Partially Exposed); Zoroaster Granite; Vishnu Schist; Proterozoic Fault.

Chuar Group (not exposed at river level): Sixtymile, Kwagunt, Galeros, Nankoweap — "These formations are not exposed at river level."

CG, N, B, S, TG, River

Rock Types
- Shale - Siltstone
- Sandstone
- Conglomerate
- Limestone - Dolomite
- Igneous
- Metamorphic

Figure 3.1
Stratigraphy of Grand Canyon region

Geologic History[293]

Metamorphic and igneous basement bedrock lies beneath the upper sedimentary strata of the southern Colorado Plateau, and these metamorphic rocks are exposed in the deepest parts of Grand Canyon. These strata are called the **Granite Gorge Metamorphic Suite** and the **Zoroaster Plutonic Complex** (Granite).[156] The gneisses and schists of the inner gorge were metamorphosed mainly between 1.84 –1.66 b.y. ago, a process of prolonged, tectonic transformation of early sedimentary and igneous strata. Tectonism drove the parent early-Proterozoic sediments and basalt flows as much as 15-25 km beneath the Earth's surface, subjecting them to temperatures of 470-840°C. The parent rock melted and recrystallized under tremendous pressures for millions of years, forming the high-grade metamorphic rocks we see today in the three Granite Gorges in the Canyon. This deformation event likely produced a major range of mountains, perhaps similar to the modern Alps.[187] Obviously, the more than 200 m.y. of time during metamorphism included multiple geologic events and changing environments, with pulses of magmatic and metamorphic activity, today revealed through cross-cutting dikes and great variation in metamorphic rock mineralogy.

What lies beneath the metamorphic basement of Grand Canyon? Karlstrom et al.[156] suggest that even older basement rock lies there, dating to Yavapai Province times, 2.5 b.y. ago, based on the age of mineral grains found in the Vishnu Schist.

The Earlier Unconformity: 1.66-1.25 b.y. ago[151]

In the 400 m.y. following metamorphism of the **Vishnu Schist**, the uplifted mountain ranges eroded away. Subsidence of the crust gradually returned the region to a beveled continent, like Australia. In Grand Canyon this phase of Earth history shows up only as an unconformity between two layers; however Quartermaster Canyon in western Grand Canyon contains schist that dates to

about 1.4 b.y., indicating that metamorphism continued well into the Mesoproterozic Era.[156]

The Middle and Late Proterozoic Grand Canyon Supergroup: 1.25 b.y.–620 m.y. ago[64a, 151, 294]

Beginning about 1.25 b.y. ago, 14,000 ft (4.3 km) of marine sediments were deposited in nine formations in eastern Grand Canyon. These strata are divided into three or four groups that had similar depositional environments. Collectively the Unkar Group, the Nankoweap/Chuar Group, and the Sixtymile Formation are known as the **Grand Canyon Supergroup**.

The **Unkar Group** is composed of five formations and, where exposed, attains a thickness of 5,320–7,200 ft (1,622-2,195 m).[17, 294] The lowermost (oldest) formation is the cliff-forming **Bass Limestone**, a 120–340 ft (37–104 m) thick gray or reddish stratum that was deposited 1.25 b.y. ago. It is a dolomitic (magnesium-bearing) limestone interbedded with sandstone and siltstone, and includes the reddish brown **Hotauta Conglomerate** as an irregular lower member. Locally distributed stromatolites (fossil algal clumps) indicate that the Bass Limestone was deposited in a shallow marine environment. Appearing first at Mile 77, the Bass Limestone has been partially metamorphosed by a dark igneous sill of diabase (a horizontal intrusion of magma between strata). This contact metamorphism produced serpentine (an ornamental stone) and long asbestos fibers prized by William Bass, John Hance, and other early miners.[21]

Overlying the Bass Limestone is the 430–830 ft (131–253 m) thick, brick-red **Hakatai Shale**, which first appears just above Hance Rapid.[17] The **Shinumo Quartzite** is first seen at Mile 75, and it attains a thickness of 1,060 to 1,560 ft (323–476 m). "Marble cake" bedding in the upper Shinumo may have been created when Proterozoic earthquakes shook the unconsolidated sediments.[54, 294]

The Bright Angel Fault, which forms Bright Angel Canyon at Mile 88, became active about 1.2 b.y. ago as or just after the Shinumo was deposited. Above the Shinumo Quartzite lies the **Dox Sandstone**, which was deposited about 1.2–1.1 b.y. ago and is 3,000 ft (914 m) thick. The Dox is easily eroded, and the Canyon opens wide when the river meets this soft, red sandstone at Mile 62.5. Uppermost in the Unkar Group is the dark, 980 ft- (299 m) thick **Cardenas Basalt**, exposed below Mile 65. Volcanic activity about 1.08 b.y. ago[71, 294] forced molten intrusions through and between Unkar Group sediments, spilling lava across the Precambrian terrain. One prominent dike (a verticle intrusion of magma) from that period may influence the position of Hance Rapid.

The **Nankoweap Formation** may be more closely related to the Chuar Group. The formation is most clearly seen in Nankoweap and Basalt Canyons (Miles 52 R and 69R, respectively). At 370 ft (113 m) thick, this purplish marine sandstone is about 800 m.y. old. It contains three unconformities but much of its geologic story is missing.

The **Chuar Group** was deposited between 800 and 742 m.y. ago and includes the 4,270 ft (1,302 m) thick **Galeros Formation**, which underlies the 1,950 ft (595 m) thick **Kwagunt Formation**.[64a] These formations consist mostly of shales and siltstones, with *Boxonia* brain stromatolites, five other genera of stromatolites, as well as *Chuaria*[64a] and many other microfossils. Neither of those formations are exposed along the river, but they are visible a short distance up Nankoweap, Carbon, and Lava Canyons (Miles 52R, 64½R, and 65½R, respectively).

The **Sixtymile Formation** is 200 ft (61 m) thick and consists of sandstone, conglomerate, and landslide materials. Exposed only on top of Nankoweap Butte and in upper Sixtymile Canyon, it was deposited about 700–620 m.y. ago and reflects geologic unrest along the Neoproterozoic Butte Fault, and perhaps globally.[64a, 78]

The Upper Portion of the Great Unconformity: 742 to 540 m.y. ago

The Grand Canyon Supergroup sediments were deposited in tectonically active basins, and after deposition the fault basins continued to be active, with as much as two vertical miles (3.1 km) of uplift along the Butte Fault.[152] Nearly all Supergroup sediments were weathered away, and the only Precambrian strata remaining from this 200-m.y. erosional episode are found in fault wedges exposed by the Colorado River and its tributaries, particularly between Miles 62 and 78, at Phantom Ranch, near the Bass Camps, and between Bedrock Canyon and Mile 138. In most of the Canyon only schist lies beneath the Cambrian Tapeats Sandstone, and nearly 1.2 b.y. of the geologic record are missing. Erosion of the Grand Canyon Supergroup was the last and second-largest of at least seven Proterozoic unconformities recorded within the Canyon's strata.[151]

The Neoproterozoic/Precambrian

Glaciation dominated the earth during at least three discrete Neoproterozoic episodes. During the Precambrian Cryogenian Period (850-635 m.y. ago), the relatively brief Kaigas glaciation event was followed by the much longer Sturtian glaciation event, which landed ice below sea level in tropical latitudes 717 m.y. ago.[179] Marinoan glaciation occurred at the conclusion of the Ediacaran Period (635-541 m.y. ago) and appears to have covered the globe with ice sheets.[5] This lends support to the notion of Huronian (2.5 b.y. ago) and late Precambrian "Snowball Earth," the recovery from which may have triggered the eruption of Cambrian multicellular life. Also, melting of the "Snowball Earth" may be responsible for the massive marine transgressions that characterized the early Cambrian Period in North America.

Paleozoic Strata: 542 to 252 m.y. ago[24, 187]

Following the erosion represented by the "Great Unconformity," deposition began on the sea floor off the coast of western North America. The 14 described Paleozoic formations in the Grand Canyon attain a total thickness of 3,500-6,500 ft (1.1-2.0 km), with all but the Tapeats and Coconino Formations increasing in thickness to the west. Unconformities of varying lengths within and between each successive age interrupt the geologic record, and the only Paleozoic periods not represented by strata in Grand Canyon are the Ordovician and Silurian Periods (485-423 m.y. ago).

Cambrian **Tonto Group** (ca. 541–505 m.y. ago) sediments were laid down sequentially during the continent-wide Sauk marine transgression (an invasion of the land by the ocean).[17, 190, 254] Lowermost in the Tonto Group is the cliff-forming **Tapeats Sandstone**, which varies in thickness from 100–325 feet (30–100 m). This layer first emerges at river level at about Mile 59.5, just upstream from the mouth of the Little Colorado River, and quickly forms dark, well-stratified walls. The Tapeats consists of three members, which Nobel[216] described in the Shinumo Quadragle (central Grand Canyon) as consisting of a 200 ft (61 m)-thick "brown slabby sandstone or pebbly grit," lying beneath a 50 ft (15 m)-thick "shaly brown or greenish sandstone," topped by a 35 ft (11 m)-thick "white cross-bedded sandstone with *scolithus*" (tubular fossil burrows of marine worms). The formation decreases in thickness from the eastern Canyon to the west, and similar sandstones are found across the U.S.

Above it and interbedded with it lies the **Bright Angel Shale**, which formed as the continental margin subsided a bit deeper into the Cambrian sea. This green and purple shale first appears at Mile 50 and increases in thickness from 300 to 450 ft (91–137 m) from east to west. Rust-colored bands of dolomitic **Muav Limestone** become more prominent in this shale to the west. The 530 m.y. old Muav Limestone and overlying **Undivided Dolomites** (age undetermined) form a steep cliff above the easily eroded, slope-forming Bright Angel Shale. The Muav first emerges from the river near Mile 35 and increases from 350–1,000 ft (107–305 m) in thickness from east to west. The **Undivided ("Undifferentiated") Dolomites** reach a thickness of 400 ft (122 m) in the west. Sequential deposition and interbedding in a complex transgressive environment obscure the contacts between these four Cambrian strata. Both the Tapeats and Bright Angel are rich in worm burrows, trilobite resting marks, and other trace fossils, but fossils of trilobites, sponges, crinoids, and other marine invertebrates are difficult to find in the Muav Limestone.

A pre-Devonian unconformity lasted 62 m.y. and is the only geologic reminder of the Ordovician and Silurian Periods (485–423 m.y. ago) in Grand Canyon. During that time the Canyon region probably underwent a regression (a retreat of the ocean's waters), and sediments that were deposited eroded away.

Devonian deposits 420-372 m.y. ago provide evidence of a major marine transgression. During this Age of Fishes, large rivers wound through the region towards the west coast, which at that time ran up through central Arizona. In Lower Marble Canyon these **Devonian river channels** are incised into the top of the Muav Limestone (e.g., just upstream from the mouth of Buck Farm Canyon at the top of the talus slope). In western Grand Canyon the Devonian sea deposited the **Temple Butte Formation**, a thin-bedded, 450 ft (137 m) thick limestone that lies directly beneath the Redwall Limestone. The Temple Butte Formation was probably deposited in a shallow, possibly inter-tidal, marine environment. At that time Grand Canyon lay near the equator. Fossils are rare in the Temple Butte, but the remains of primitive fish have been collected.

The **Redwall Formation** was deposited by a shallow tropical sea during transgressions in the first half of the Mississippian Period (359–331 m.y. ago).[28a, 189] Increasing in thickness from 540–700 ft (165–213 m) from east to west, the sheer Redwall cliff first emerges at Mile 23 and is composed of four members. Lowermost is the Whitmore Wash Member, a light gray limestone and dolomite bed, underlying the Thunder Springs Member with its alternating light and dark bands of carbonate, dolomite, and chert. Third up is the thick, pure limestone of the Mooney Falls Member. Uppermost is the Horseshoe Mesa Member, a thin-bedded, light gray limestone that forms ledges. Redwall Limestone is actually ivory colored, with black dolomitic bands: its red color is due to iron oxide (rust) stains that leach down from upper strata. "Desert varnish," a black manganese oxide, also commonly stains the Canyon's walls.

The Redwall, like other limestones, is composed largely of calcium carbonate ($CaCO_3$), deposited as a precipitate and also as shell-bearing marine organisms died and drifted to the sea floor. Fossils from the Redwall include sponges, crinoids (sea lillies), brachiopods, dome and horn corals, and both straight and coiled nautiloids.[156, 189] Chert, a silicious mineral derived from sponges (biogenic opal) and other sources, is abundant in the lower Redwall as nodules and veins. Chert may have formed as blue-green algal mats were preferentially silicified in tidal or subtidal waters.[28a] Chert was widely used for making arrowheads by Native Americans. Numerous caves exist in the Redwall, and the formation serves as an important regional aquifer, feeding most of the major, cool-water springs of Grand Canyon. Both the North and South Rims obtain drinking water from Roaring Springs near the head of Bright Angel Creek.

Channel lenses of late Mississippian **Surprise Canyon Formation** lie at the top of the Redwall,[18] with the best exposures visible from river level on the right as you run 24 ½ Mile Rapid and just upstream of Fern Glen (Mile 168). Recent data reveal that the late Mississippian Surprise Canyon Formation and the Pennsylvania and Permian strata in Grand Canyon contain one b.y. old grains derived from continental-scale rivers draining the Appalachian Mountains.[100]

The **Supai Group** was deposited in marine embayments during the Pennsylvanian and early Permian Periods between 323 and about 286 m.y. ago. Formerly considered a single formation, the Supai Group is actually composed of four formations.[188] With a combined thickness ranging from 950–1,350 ft (290–412 m), these sandstone and shale redbeds are separated by thin basal conglomerates (a cemented matrix of worn stones) and substantial unconformities. First seen at Soap Creek Rapid at Mile 11, the four formations are (from bottom to top) the **Watahomigi**, **Manakacha**, **Wescogame**, and **Esplanade**. The lower two strata are difficult to distinguish in Marble Canyon.[15b] Primitive reptile tracks are commonly found in the upper half of the Supai Group, and root casts of Pennsylvanian and Permian plants are found throughout those formations.

The **Hermit Shale** was deposited in a large river floodplain during the early Permian Period between 299 and 254 m.y. ago. This soft red shale, which merges with the Esplanade Formation, first appears just above Badger Rapid. It increases in thickness from 250 to more than 1,000 ft (76–305 m) from east to west. At least 35 species of ferns and other plant fossils, as well as some insects, have been collected from this easily-eroded, slope-forming shale layer.[187]

Coconino Sandstone, a buff-colored, cliff-forming stratum, first emerges at Mile 4. More than 350 ft (107 m) thick in eastern Grand Canyon, this crossbedded sandstone disappears to the west.[17] Worm and reptile tracks are common in the Coconino, indicating that deposition occurred in a terrestrial dune-dominated environment near sea level.[187]

The **Toroweap Formation** was deposited during a mid-Permian transgression/regression event. This silty limestone first emerges near Mile 2 and increases in thickness from 250–450 ft (76–137 m) from east to west. The Toroweap is composed of three members: at the bottom is the Seligman Member, a red and yellow silty sandstone that is 45 ft (14 m) thick; in the middle is the gray, cliff-forming, limestone-dolomitic Brady Canyon Member, which is up to 280 ft (85 m) thick and is rich in marine fossils; and at the top is the red and white sand-siltstone, limestone, and gypsum-bearing Woods Ranch Member, which is 180 ft (55 m) thick.

The **Kaibab Formation**, a cream-colored, blocky limestone, appears just above the Paria Riffle (Mile 0.8L), where it immediately begins to form a sheer cliff. It is 330–600 ft (100–183 m) thick, and is composed of two members: the gray, fossil-bearing cherty Fossil Mountain Member (250–300 ft, 76–91 m thick), lying below the 80–300 ft (24–91 m) thick Harrisburg Member, which thins eastward and has alternating red and yellow mudstone, sandstone, limestone, and dolomite beds. More than 80 genera of Permian marine invertebrates, a remarkable trove of paleo-sharks[132] and other fish fossils have been collected from this formation[187] and, like the other formations down to the Surprise Canyon Formation, it contains zircon grains derived from the Appalachian Mountains. During the Permian Period Grand Canyon lay just north of the equator[28a] and the continents had converged to form the supercontinent, Pangaea. Today, the Kaibab Limestone forms the caprock of the Grand Canyon region and serves as a minor regional aquifer with good water quality.

Mesozoic Geology: 252 to 66 m.y. ago

The Paleozoic Era abruptly ended with the Earth's largest extinction event 252.3 m.y. ago. More than 95% of marine species and 70% of terrestrial vertebrate species went extinct, including 83% of all genera and 57% of all families. Causes are related to massive volcanic eruptions in Siberia, enormous releases of CO_2 and methane, global warming, massive releases of hydrogen sulfide from the ocean, decreased oceanic pH, and/or a massive meteorite impact.[15a] Life's recovery from this event took more than 10 m.y. During subsequent Triassic time, the Canyon region was uplifted as North America broke away from Laurasia (Eurasia and North America), the northern portion of Pangaea. Permian seas were replaced by Triassic lowlands between 252 and 201 m.y. ago, and 4000–8,000 ft (1.2–2.4 km) of Mesozoic sediments were deposited on top of the Kaibab Limestone. As those sediments accrued, the region slowly subsided, resulting in little net change in elevation relative to sea level. By the end of the Mesozoic Era (66 m.y.a.), the Kaibab Limestone lay 4000 ft (1220 m) below the surface, two miles (3.2 km) lower than its present elevation.

Most of the Mesozoic sediments have eroded away along the Canyon's rims,[28] but the Lees Ferry area offers excellent exposures of these Grand Staircase strata[226] and reveals a complex recent river history.[130, 224] At the launch ramp one can see the whitish, resistant **Shinarump Conglomerate**, which angles up steeply in the downstream direction, and rests atop the Triassic **Moenkopi Formation** (the shaley Chocolate Cliffs). Above the Shinarump lies a muddy sandstone and the distinctive light gray and green Chinle ("chin-lee") Shale. Together the conglomerate, sandstone, and shale make up the 100–1,150 ft (30–350 m) thick Triassic **Chinle Formation**. Above this formation at the base of the Vermilion and Echo Cliffs are the **Moenave** and **Kayenta Formations**. The upper two thirds of these escarpments, and all of Glen Canyon above Lees Ferry, is composed of the 1,400–1,700 ft (427–518 m) thick **Navajo Sandstone**, a magnificently cross-bedded early Jurassic (201–145 m.y. ago) eolian deposit. Above the Navajo Sandstone but scarcely visible at Lees Ferry are the **Carmel** and **Entrada Sandstones** of the 1,000 ft (305 m) thick Jurassic **San Rafael Group**, underlying the 100 ft (30 m) thick Cretaceous **Dakota Sandstone**.

Mesozoic fossils from the Chinle and Moenave Formations include extensive petrified forests, lungfish, crocodilian-like archosaurs, and numerous small to large dinosaurs. Only 4 in (10 cm)-long, the shrew-like *Morganucodon* has been collected from Mesozoic beds in northern Arizona and Europe. It was among the oldest known mammals, and has been found in the Triassic Kayenta Formation.[148]

Landscape Evolution of the Grand Canyon

Paleogeographic Illustrations by Ron Blakey (www.cpgeosystems.com)

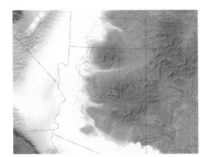

Early Cambrian
525 Ma

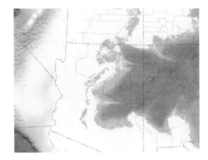

Middle-Late Cambrian
505 Ma

Late Devonian
370 Ma

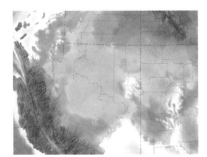

Early Permian
278 Ma

Middle Permian
270 Ma

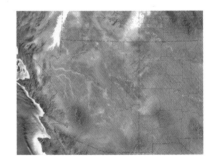

Late Permian
252 Ma

Middle Mississippian
340 Ma

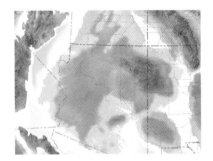

Middle Pennsylvanian
307 Ma

Early Jurrasic
180 Ma

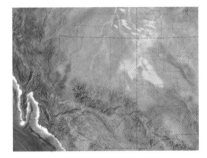

Late Jurrassic
153 Ma

Plate Tectonics

North America has not always been "north" nor recognizably "America," having been embedded in supercontinents at least three times, and each of the region's three big packets of strata mentioned above developed in relation to the assembly and break-up of a different supercontinent. Tectonic forces push the Earth's 12 large plates and more than 20 small plates across the globe at rates of 1–3 inches (2–7 cm)/yr. Supercontinents form about every 0.75 b.y., last about 100 m.y., and perhaps reform at about 90° angles to each other through a process dubbed "orthoversion."[207] Supercontinent **Columbia (Nuna)** formed from 1.8–1.5 b.y. ago, as Grand Canyon's metamorphic/crystalline basement rock formed. The Supercontinent **Rodinia**, formed as the Precambrian Grand Canyon Supergroup was deposited 1.1–0.75 b.y. ago, a time when Australia, the Antarctic, and the Mohave Desert were juxtaposed. The most recent supercontinent, **Pangaea**, was centered on the equator, assembled by about 300–200 m.y. ago as the Canyon's late Paleozoic and Triassic strata were being deposited. The next supercontinent, "**Amasia**," will assemble across the Northern Hemisphere in 300–400 m.y.[207]

THE COLORADO RIVER AND THE PAST 75 MILLION YEARS

Overview

For all of its magnificence as a landform, Grand Canyon is a relatively recent surface feature etched into the face of far older rocks. The strata through which the river cuts reveal 40% of Earth's history, but the Colorado River drainage and the Grand Canyon have only developed over the past 75 m.y., and the Colorado is just one of many great rivers that have cut across this region over geologic time. Late in the Cretaceous Period (145–66 m.y. ago) the Kaibab Limestone had 4,000-8,000 ft (1,220–2,440 m) of younger strata on top of it and lay 4,000–8,000 ft below the surface. Today this rock layer is the capstone of the southern Colorado Plateau, reaching 9,100 ft (2,775 m) elevation on the North Rim. This means that the Kaibab Formation has risen at least 13,000 ft (nearly 4 km) in the past 75 m.y. during several uplift events. Collectively, these uplifts caused regional erosion during what Clarence Dutton called "the Great Denudation," today leaving us the Grand Staircase of the Colorado Plateau, with Grand Canyon's metamorphic rocks as its basement steps.

The Colorado Plateau is a micro-tectonic plate that has remained enigmatically unaltered during Phaenerozoic time. It rose more-or-less undeformed through Cretaceous and Cenozoic tectonic activity that shaped western North America. Late in the process of uplift, the Colorado River's course became integrated, but in a puzzling way. The river cuts through, rather than around, major upwarps, including the Kaibab and Hualapai/Shivwits Plateaus, seemingly in defiance of gravity. Its present course is only partially controlled by north-trending faults (Fig. 3.3).[152, 154] It sub-parallels the East Kaibab Monocline between Marble Canyon and Tanner Rapid, and follows the Hurricane Fault swarm for 35 mi (56 km) downstream to Diamond Creek, but elsewhere follows no fault system faithfully. Clearly, the development of the river's course has been a complex process.

Controversy over how and when Grand Canyon formed has raged for more than a century,[77, 154, 157, 191, 293, 341] engagingly reviewed by Ranney.[236] Here we'll entangle ourselves in the timing, causes, recent orogenies, the hows and whens of a river assuming drainage dominance in the Southwest, and Grand Canyon's emergence as a recognizable landform. Table 3.2 summarizes critical geologic events in late Cretaceous and throughout the Cenozoic Period from 75 m.y. ago to the present.

River Basin Development

Rivers develop through several potentially interacting processes, of which John Wesley Powell described three. *Consequent* channels develop as uplift occurs and rivers run down the side of the uplift: Hunt[140] reported evidence of an early Cenozoic river west of the newly risen Rocky Mountains in the upper Colorado River basin. Powell[230] and Walcott[318] described the process of *superimposition,* in which a downcutting river exposes an uplifted block and cuts through it. This phenomenon is abundantly observed in exposures of "islands" of Precambrian Grand Canyon Supergroup sediments in the upper half of Grand Canyon. Lastly, *antecedent* channels are in place prior to uplift, and the river incises as uplift occurs. Powell[230] generally favored antecedence as the leading mechanism for development of the Colorado River's course. Pederson[223a] recently evaluated the river's history of base elevation change in eastern Grand Canyon, reporting an es-

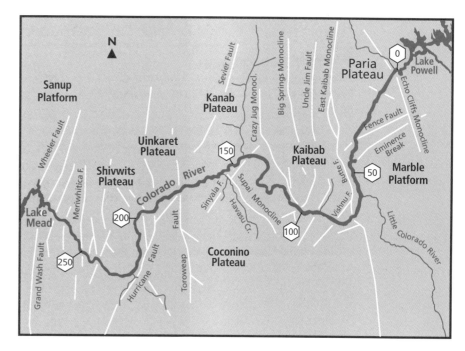

Figure 3.2
Major faults in the Grand Canyon region.

Table 3.2

Major late Cretaceous and Cenozoic geologic events and climate changes that influenced the Grand Canyon region, 75 m.y. ago to the present.

75–40 m.y. ago

Laramide Orogeny (74–40 m.y. ago) compressional faulting elevates the Rocky Mountains;[152] closure of the North American Interior seaway; reverse faulting on Butte and other faults, and west-side-up compression on western Grand Canyon faults; uplift of Pacific coast elevates western Grand Canyon,[332] creating a northeast-flowing "California River,"[64] removing Permian and Pennsylvanian strata, and possibly incision near present levels in the western Canyon;[332] uplifted Mogollon Highlands with drainage to the north and east onto Colorado Plateau 65–55 m.y. ago;[323] Hindu fanglomerate from SW Utah deposited across the Colorado River's present-day course on Hualapai Plateau 60–50 m.y. ago;[340] a lake/marshy lowland occupies the Four Corners area (San Juan Basin) and develops interior drainage; a drainage network begins to develop west of Rocky Mountains;[140] Colorado Plateau begins rising to <30% of its modern elevation;[66, 152] Apatite 4He/3He and (U-TH)/He evidence suggests that the early Colorado River incorporated one or more ancient canyons in the development of its course. [96,157a,157b]

35–15 m.y. ago

"Ignimbrite flare-up" with massive explosive felsic magmatic activity[152] was likely accompanied by additional surface uplift of the region due to mantle-driving forces. Older paleocanyons were partly filled by small, locally-sourced river sediments; Oligocene rivers (Buck and Doe conglomerate) sourced with local debris eroded from Permian and Pennsylvania strata of western Grand Canyon in Diamond Creek and Milkweed Canyon drainages.[340]

21 m.y. ago–present

Basin and Range Orogeny elevates Sierra Nevada and creates hundreds of smaller, north-trending ranges throughout the Intermountain West; eastern Grand Canyon partially incised across the Kaibab uplift (at an erosion level below the Kaibab Limestone surface), as shown by thermochronology data.[157, 171]

18–13 m.y. ago

Drainage onto western side of the Plateau in the Lower Basin, with little topograhic relief along SW margin of Colorado Plateau 18 m.y. ago;[342] Basin and Range extensional rifting and spreading along the Grand Wash Fault most active 18–16 m.y. ago, creating deep, west-side-down trenches.[174, 175] Drainage reversal on southern Colorado Plateau from the NE towards the S-SW (Peach Springs Tuff) into Hurricane Fault zone and SW Utah basins.[92, 215a,340] No through-flowing Colorado River in Lower Basin;[174] magmatism shifts from felsic to basaltic after 15 Ma; rain shadow desert develops across the Intermountain West as Basin and Range mountains rise.

13–5.7 m.y. ago

Displacement along SW edge of Colorado Plateau in Grand Wash develops through extension by 9 m.y. ago, controlled by the diffuse, north-trending boundary between Early Proterozoic crustal provinces;[91] **Muddy Creek Formation** develops as trenches along SW corner of the Plateau and fill with more than 10,000 ft (3,000 m) of locally-derived erosional outwash sediments but not derived from the Colorado River; [157, 223] Lake Bidahochi forms 13–6 m.y. ago, but no evidence of flow reversal of the Little Colorado River drainage; mid-Miocene?

Crooked Ridge River flows from SW Colorado southward across Grand Canyon region;[176a] Gulf of California opens 8–6 m.y. ago, initiating integration of Lower Colorado River drainage. Although an upper Colorado River is present in its present course near Grand Junction, Colorado ca. 10 m.y. ago, no through-flowing Colorado River exists in Lake Mead area at 6 m.y. ago;[157, 223] Lower Colorado River Basin rising;[172-173] 750–900 m vertical displacement on normal faults across Grand Canyon region after 6 m.y.

5.6-3.8 m.y. ago.
Canyon cutting occurs in western Grand Canyon; Colorado River sediments detected in Grand Wash Trough after 5.6 m.y. ago, and in Salton Sea Trough 5.3 m.y. ago.[71] Oldest known Colorado River gravels underlie a 4.4 m.y. old basalt flow at Sandy Point on Lake Mead;[92] consistent incision rates over the past 4 m.y. and extrapolated to 6 million yr are sufficient to incise much of Grand Canyon;[152] desertification of Southwest in early-middle Pliocene as regional rain shadow develops.

3.8-3.3 m.y. ago
Through-flowing Colorado river in its present course is well developed in western Grand Canyon; Colorado and Kaibab Plateaus near present elevation; Hurricane Fault active from 3.5 Ma to present and Toroweap Fault active after 3 m.y. ago and mantle-driven Colorado Plateau uplift.[152] Land bridge develops between North and South America, with mammalian predators invading southward, and South American flora and fauna moving northward (the American Southwest shares about 150 plant and animal genera with central-western South America). [180a,335a]

3.2-0.75 m.y. ago
Pleistocene Epoch—glaciers form in mountains in Intermountain West, but not on most of the Colorado Plateau; climate is cooler, more humid.

<0.75-0.2 m.y. ago
Ice ages continue; lava flows near Mile 179 dam the river, with one or more catastrophic outburst floods;[94,95] Hurricane Fault active;[152] multiple large slope failure events throughout Grand Canyon where Bright Angel Shale meets river; lacustrine silty-sand deposits in Grand Canyon caves at 4,000 ft (1,220 m) elevation;[79] clearwater inundation of Stantons Cave by a natural dam downstream leaves a pile of driftwood more than 43 k.y. old, but no river-derived sand or silt.[84]

20-13 k.y. ago
No evidence of exceptionally large Pleistocene floods, as shown by 15,000 yr (k.y.)-old packrat middens within 200 ft (60 m) of river level at lower Bass Camp area. Climate transition from Pleistocene to Holocene, initiates strong summer monsoons; 3,000 ft (1,000 m) upslope shift of life zones occurs with desertification of Southwest; humans arrive in Southwest, Pleistocene megafaunal extinction by about 12,000 years ago.[95a,182a]

13 k.y. ago–1935 Contemporary Era
Desertification advances; largest known flood, 350,000 cfs occurred ca. 1,400 yr ago;[130, 219] global warming initiated by human activities but transmission of European diseases in the New World after 1492 sets off Little Ice Age (1400–1880). [213] Largest historic flood, 1884.

1935
Hoover Dam completed; Lake Mead first filled to capacity in 1941.[129, 268]

1963
Glen Canyon Dam completed (Chapter VI)[181]

The Lava Falls Volcanic Field

Two dikes (sheet-like intrusions of rock) snake their way up through the Paleozoic strata near Mile 159. A large plug of lava is visible in the Muav limestone high above the river near Mile 178L, and travertine springs and large, menacing "lava-cados" perch along the river. Another dike works its way skyward at Vulcan's Anvil (Mile 178). Below the Anvil, massive rivers of lava repeatedly flowed into the Canyon over the last 750,000 years, particularly from the Toroweap Valley, Old Whitmore Wash, and Prospect Canyon. Of the many vents and cinder cones that roost along both rims, the largest is the 760 ft- (232 m) tall Vulcans Throne, directly above Lava Falls. Looking upstream from Mile 182, it is just visible on the north side of the river. New geologic data on this volcanic field has renewed debate over the dynamism of Grand Canyon's recent history.

The Lava Falls volcanic field is the easternmost and youngest of the three volcanic fields in western Grand Canyon. It produced the spectacular lava flows noted by Powell[230] and subsequently studied. Flows extend 50 mi (80 km) north, encompassing 17 flows and totaling 4.75 mi^3 (22 km^3) of magma. Four groups of flows are distinguished by viscosity, mineralogy, and cross-cutting geometries.[60]

More than a dozen of these flows erupted within, or poured into the Canyon from eight…

timated incision rate of 142 m/m.y., a rate sufficient for antecedence. A new twist on antecedence involves regional epeirogeny where the western Colorado Plateau may have been uplifted at semi-steady rates by dynamic mantle processes.[179]

Both antecedence and superimposition interactively influence the development of each major segment of the river, prompting Hunt[140] to propose the process of *anteposition*, in which an antecedent river is superimposed onto exposed geologic structure. Another channel-forming mechanism is *drainage capture,* a mechanism of basin expansion through which the most actively eroding drainage basin acquires the flow of adjacent streams, increasing the pirating stream's erosional capacity. One other process that generates stream channels is *lake overflow*. For example, 17,400 m.y. ago, a high Pleistocene stage of the 20,000 mi^2 (51,778 km^2) Lake Bonneville—the gigantic ancestor of the modern-day Great Salt Lake—resulted in release of nearly 1,000 mi^3 (4,165 km^3) of water in a massive outwash flood through Red Rock Pass into the Snake River in northern Utah and Idaho. Progressive overflow also has been suggested[196, 262] but rejected[67] as a mechanism linking east- and west-side drainages across the Kaibab Plateau. Nevertheless, several channel development mechanisms likely played a role in the development of the Colorado River's course over Cenozoic time.

The late Cretaceous-early Cenozoic Laramide Orogeny (mountain building event) was a period of geologic compression that elevated the Rocky Mountains, reactivating long-quiescent late Precambrian and Paleozoic faults. The eastern Pacific Farallon Plate was subducted (over-ridden) by western North America. During Laramide time, the angle of subduction shallowed, creating lateral pressures far inland at the ancient Rocky Mountain Cordilleran plate boundary, and causing uplift.[66, 68, 81, 147] This drove up the Rocky Mountains, reactivated the Proterozoic Butte, Bright Angel, and other faults (reversing the direction of faulting), and may have caused uplift and monoclinal folding across the southern Plateau. Early in Cenozoic time the Plateau was still vested with 4,000-8,000 ft of relatively soft and easily erodible Mesozoic and early Cenozoic sedimentary strata, into which drainages began to develop.[140] However, those drainages likely were flowing to the northeast.

Continued or punctuated uplift of the Plateau continued to occur after Laramide time, with widespread volcanic activity. The Basin and Range Orogeny (21 m.y. to the present) began extensional faulting, uplifting and pulling apart the Earth's crust in the Basin and Range Geologic Province, including Nevada, eastern California, western Utah, southeastern Oregon, southern Arizona and New Mexico, western Texas, and northern Mexico. This extensional orogeny occurred as the Pacific Farallon Plate was pushed (subducted) beneath North America, and melted or sank, perhaps opening a window of rising magma beneath the Intermountain West.[152] Uplift and extensional deformation caused well-developed drainages, such as the Salt River in central Arizona, to reverse flow direction.[228b]

The Lower Colorado River drainage and southern Colorado Plateau reveal details of developmental chronology not available upstream.[174, 175] The Basin and Range orogeny halted northward flow across the Hualapai Plateau after 17 m.y. ago, and after 12 m.y. ago created deep fault trenches and north-trending extensional horst and graben valleys that today dominate the Intermountain West. Immediately west of Grand Canyon in the Lake Mead area, these deep Basin and Range trenches filled with Muddy Creek Formation sediments between 11-6 m.y. ago. However, extensive research has revealed no Colorado River sediments in the Muddy Creek strata,[23, 223] indicating that the Colorado River was not yet present. The earliest Colorado River sediments found downstream from Grand Canyon occur in the Grand Wash Trough at about 6 m.y. ago,[262a] and were deposited in the Salton Trough about 5.3 m.y. ago.[64, 65] While flow reversal

…sources. These flows created basalt dams of various heights, and one flow was sufficiently fluid to travel more than 73 mi (117 km) downstream.[116–117]

Lava flows produce a suite of basalt strata based on cooling time.[171a] Uppermost in many Grand Canyon region flows is a *vesicular* (gas cavity) *stratum* that cools rapidly, forming a sharp-edged crust. Rapid cooling creates a thick *upper entablature* of joints and pentagonal or hexagonal basalt columns 1 ft (30 cm) or less in diameter. Convection or infiltrating water may generate radiating patterns (e.g., visable about Mile 184R). At the bottom, slower cooling produces the wider columns of the *basal colonnade*. A *basal vesicular stratum* also may form if the lava flows across cool or moist ground.

River cobbles beneath the basalt flows just upstream from Lava Falls and across from Hells Hollow (Mile 183R) indicate that the Colorado River had cut to near its present depth by 500,000 yr ago. Larger lava dams may have created reservoirs dozens to hundreds of miles in length, which may have persisted long enough for their basins to fill with sediment.[60, 116] Overflow allowed the river to shift its channel off to the side of the basalt flows.[230] At Miles 183R, 194L, and elsewhere the river cut entirely new channels, leaving old, lava- and gravel-filled beds perched off to the side of the river's present-day course.

Concluding Mysteries

Provocative, unexplained questions and issues surround the Canyon's geologic history. For example, 1) Why do silty lake deposits occur up to 4,000 ft (1,220 m) elevation in upper Canyon caves?[79] 2) Are all of the Canyon's massive travertine deposits (upstream from the Little Colorado River on the left, in Travertine and Bass Canyons, and at Royal Arch Creek) roughly the same age?[59, 159] 3) Are all of the major slumps along the river similar in age, including those at Nankoweap, along the lower Little Colorado River, downstream from Fossil Canyon (Mile 125 area), in the Tapeats-Deer Creek corridor,[240] and at Red Slide (Mile 177R) and related to (2) by climate and/or by natural dams? 4) The river's course clearly was deflected by the Eminence Fault (which may be an extension of the Proterozoic Bright Angel Fault), forming one of the world's deepest, incised river meanders between Miles 41 and 46. Was the Eminence Fault an important escarpment across the region early in the Colorado River's history? 5) Why does the apparently young (5.3 m.y.-old) lower Canyon look so much older than the canyon upstream? These and other intriguing questions continue to enliven the geolocgical debate over the origins and history of Grand Canyon.

occurred along the southern edge of the Colorado Plateau, no evidence of Colorado Plateau sediments occur in Pliocene Lake Bidahochi, indicating that the Little Colorado River did not reverse its flow direction.

During and following uplift associated with the Basin and Range Orogeny, the Colorado River developed and integrated its present path, capturing and incising their canyons prior to Grand Canyon and, by 5.3 m.y. ago, had become the dominant drainage system of the Southwest.[157, 228a] River cobbles beneath lava flows near Miles 179 and 183 indicate that the Canyon reached nearly its current depth there by 0.75–0.5 m.y. ago. Incision rates in eastern Grand Canyon are estimated at 143 to 250–411 m/m.y. and 50–123 m/m.y. west of the Hurrican Fault.[59, 152, 228]

Support for a youthful Canyon that incised to its present depth in less than 6 m.y.,[152, 174-176] but linking older paleocanyon segments from earlier landscapes.[96, 131, 140, 332, 157b] We live in an age of erosion, in which the forces that created the Colorado River's course and Grand Canyon have removed most of the geological record of their geomorphic evolution. Rather than simply "young" or "old," the Colorado River appears to have developed its present course over a relatively short period of time, in relation to earlier drainages or alignments. Thus the process has involved complex, regional-to-more-localized tectonism and channel formation mechanisms, which likely operated at different times and to differing extents among channel segments. The integration of the river's course has provided egress for 74,420 mi^3 (310,000 km^3) of the Earth's crust from the Colorado Plateau,[70] perhaps unweighting the Plateau and allowing it to rebound (rise) and erode even more rapidly over time. Numerous lines of evidence, new geochronology tools and data, and a more sophisticated understanding of Cretaceous and Cenzoic events are gradually revealing a unified geologic landscape history.[293]

IV. HUMAN HISTORY IN GRAND CANYON

Introduction

The America Southwest has been peopled by Native American cultures for more than 11,000 yr, through four periods of prehistory and historic times: the **Paleoindian Period** (9200—8300 years before the current era, BCE), the several phases of the **Archaic Period** (ca. 8300—ca. 1000 BCE), the **Preformative Period** (ca. 1000 BCE—500 years current era, CE), the **Formative Period** (500–1250 CE), and the **Late Prehistoric/Protohistoric Period** (1250—1776 CE). Southwestern prehistory has been studied intensively in the Grand Canyon region.[88] Several prehistoric cultures disappeared (e.g., Paleoindian, Archaic, and Cohonina cultures), while other cultures developed or immigrated into the region over time. The modern Hopi and Zuni Indians trace their ancestry to now-vanished Uto-Aztecan Basketmaker and Ancestral Pueblo (also called Hisatsinom—the Hopi name for their ancestors), Sinagua, Fremont, and other Cultures, while archeological and linguistic evidence shows that the Pai, Paiute, and Navajo Cultures colonized the region from widely different origination points during the Late Prehistoric/Protohistoric Periods (Figs. 4.1, 4.2). Today, five tribes occupy reservation lands in or immediately around the Canyon (the Hopi, Havasupai, Hualapai, Navajo, and the Kaibab Band of the Southern Paiute), and the Zuni, Southern Ute, and others additionally claim cultural affinity with it. In 1540 CE, a small band of Spanish conquistadores lead by Captain Garcia Lopez de Cárdenas, was the first group of Europeans to view Grand Canyon, beginning the **Historic Period**. From prehistoric to recent times, Grand Canyon has exerted a profound socio-cultural influence over all those who live in and around it. Table 4.1 provides a summary of the human history of the Colorado River in Grand Canyon.

Figure 4.1

Distribution of Formative Period cultures around the Grand Canyon region, 700-1500 CE. Adapted from Fairley 2003: Figure 40 (courtesy of Statistical Research, Inc.).[88]

"Tovar learned of a great river to the west, and returned to report to Coronado at Zuni. A month later Coronado sent the army-master Garcia Lopez de Cárdenas back to Hopi, to pick up guides to take them to the great river. After they had gone twenty days they came to the banks of the river, which seemed no more than three or four leagues above the stream which flowed between them...They spent three days on this bank looking for a passage down to the river, which looked from above as if the water was 6 feet across, although the Indians said it was half a league wide."

Winship 1896[335a]

Human History Timeline

9200–8300 BC	**Paleoindian Period**: No evidence of Clovis Cluture (9,200–8,900 BCE); possible Folsom Culture 8,900–8,300 BCE spear-point fragment in GC.[6,88,90,126,127,128,182,182a]
8300–1000 BCE	**Archaic Period**: Red Butte site Early Archaic; Late Archaic willow split-twig figurines in GC caves (2870–1485 BCE), Marble Canyon hearth (2289–2508 BCE), campsite charcoal (1260–410 BCE). Maize (corn) agriculture in southern AZ began by 2100 BCE, but not in northern Arizona. [57,80,88,90,130a, 178,203,219]
1000 BCE–500 CE	**Preformative Period**: Evidence of humans only from hearths.[88,90]
500–700 CE two	**Early Formative Period**: Evidence of pre-Puebloan Basketmaker Culture in GC limited to hearths, pots, plant fragments. [88,90]
700–1250	**Mid-Late Formative Period**: Puebloan Anasazi (Hisatsinom) appear in GC after 700 CE. Kayenta Anasazi in eastern GC and Four Corners area, constructed communities at Anasazi Bridge, Nankoweap, Unkar, and Bright Angel, Tapeats, and Deer Creeks. Virgin River Anasazi sites are widley scattered across western GC, with biggest settlement at the "Lost City" on Overton Arm of Lake Mead. Cohonina Culture on South Rim with a more diffuse culture and like Anasazi were active traders. Sinagua Culture south of GC and Fremont Culture to north. GC abandonned after 1150 CE probably due to drought. [56b,72a,76,85,88,90,153,177,186,197,248,249,251,305]
1250–1539 and	**Early Protohistoric Period**: Beamer Cabin built in LCR mouth rockshelter on top of 1300 CE Hopi earlier Native American archeological site. Yman Pai (Hualapai, Havasupai) arrive in GC area from southwest. Paiute arrive on north side of river from the west. Athabascan Navajo arrive after about 1500 CE from central Canada.[88,90,149a]
1540	**Historic Period**: Captain Garcia Lopez de Cárdenas reaches South Rim.[335a]
1680	Pueblo revolt against Spanish, Hopi revolt against Spanish re-colonization in 1700–01.[29a, 49a]
1776	Father Francisco Garces visits Supai. Francisco Atanasio Domínguez and Silvestre Vélez de Escalante (Spanish priests) seek a route from Santa Fe, NM to San Francisco, CA, passing thorugh the upper Green River, Utah Lake, and Arizona Strip areas, fording the Colorado River at "The Crossing of the Fathers" near Hite, UT.[322a]
1826	James Ohio Pattie party walks along South Rim, reaching the river near Lees Ferry (?)[222]
1850–1870	Jacob Hamblin, the "Buckskin Apostle" locates Lees Ferry, meets Ives Expedition in 1858, and John Wesley Powell in 1870.[137,242,335b]

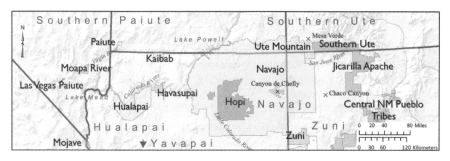

Figure 4.2
Distribution of Historic Period Native American cultures around the Grand Canyon region after 1600 CE. Adapted from Fairley 2003: Figure 40 (courtesy of Statistical Research, Inc.).[88]

1857	John D. Lee is one of several leaders of the southwestern Utah Mountain Meadow Massacre of 120 Arkansas pioneers in the Baker-Fancher party.[32]
1857–1858	Lt. Joseph Ives runs "The Explorer" steamboat to head of navigation near Hoover Dam, hitting a rock. Their party marches overland, down Diamond Creek to the river, and across South Rim to Ft. Defiance.[137,139]
1867	James White reaches Callville, Nevada, having run part of the Colorado River on a log raft after his partners were killed by Indians or drowned.[169,264]
1868	Navajo Indian Reservation is established.
1869	One-armed Civil War veteran John Wesley Powell (1834–1902) runs first intentional exploration of Colorado River from Green River, Wyoming through Grand Canyon, 24 May–30 August. Three men leave the expedition at Separation Canyon and disappear, probably killed by Paiute Indians. One of America's most influential scientists, Powell became the second director of the US Geological Survey (1881–1894) and headed the Bureau of Ethnology.[56,74,137,169,230,234, 266,280]
1871–1872	Powell's second trip through Grand Canyon ends at Kanab Creek on 7 September. Lees Ferry is established by excommunicated but still loyal Mormon John D. Lee. Lee had been sent to the ferry area by Brigham Young. Lee was arrested in 1874, convicted in 1876, executed by military shooting in 1877. Emma (Lee's 17th of 19 wives) takes over ferry operations. The Wheeler Expedition attempts to up-travel the Colorado River, ending trip at Diamond Creek.[32a,32b,137,242,266]
1877	Zuni Indian Reservation is esstablished.
1876	Harrison Pearce establishes Pearce's Ferry.[137]

Wheeler Expedition – Black Cañon, Colorado River, looking upstream from camp 8, 1871.

Mariott Library, University of Utah

Preston Nutter, on his fast-walking mule "Coalie" was a successful businessman and cattle rancher, across vast areas of Utah, Colorado, and Arizona. In 1893, he drove 5,000 head of cattle and grazed then on the AZ Strip (Arizona land north of the Colorado River) where he acquired water rights ro most of the springs. Nutter constructed the Whitmore Trail, and, later in life, co-authored the Taylor Grazing Act (1934) which established federal control over public rangelands by the BLM. Nutter rode mules because he said a "horse will go beyond his endurance. A mule knows his limitations and when to stop. He has more sense than a horse and some men."

1880	Ben Beamer settles at Little Colorado River. George McCormick operates McCormick's Mine (Mile 165L) near base of Seth Tanner's trail until 1907.[21]
1882	Havasupai and Hopi Indian Reservations are established.[137]
1883	Captain John Hance prospects, mines, and brings in tourists on South Rim. Hance was later supported by the Fred Harvey Company until his death in 1919. Stagecoach reaches mouth of Diamond Creek. Krakatoa erupts in Indonesia causing snow in NYC in July.[7,21,137] Hualapai Indian Reservation is established. William Wallace Bass settles Bass/Shinumo area, builds stage road to Williams and Ash Fork, and cablecar across river at Mile 108. Bass marries Ada Diefendorf and raises 4 children at Bass Point. His tourist operations were bought out by the Santa Fe Railroad in 1923 and he eventually moved to Wickenburg, dying in 1933. His ashes were scattered across Bass Tomb (Holy Grail Temple).[21,137]
1884	Flood of record (~210,000 cfs) from Krakatoa-derived snowmelt in Rocky Mountains. Farlee Hotel opens in lower Peach Springs Wash, operates until 1889.[137,219,295]
1889–1890	The Brown-Stanton party begins a summertime survey of GC for a river level railroad. President Brown, and boatmen Hansbrough, and Richards drown in upper Marble Canyon. Stanton stores gear, hikes out, and returns with better equipment, finishing the expedition in 1890. He takes hundreds of photographs of the river corridor. The railroad was never funded, and Stanton turned to prospecting and writing about Grand Canyon history.[137,169,264,265,325] Bucky O'Neill crosses at Lees Ferry in pursuit of train robbers.
1891	Miner Louis Boucher, the "hermit" of Hermit Canyon builds trail, mines, brings in tourists.[21,137]
1896	Flavell and Montez make a single boat trapping run through Grand Canyon (no beaver taken).[95b]
1897	Nathaniel Galloway, a Utah trapper, and Richmond run through Grand Canyon using flat-bottomed wooden boats, inventing stern-first technique of rowing rapids.[69,137]
1901	The dreams of former Prescott Sheriff Buckey O'Neill and East Coast investors are realized with completion of Atchison, Topeka & Santa Fe Railroad line to South Rim.[290]
1903	David Rust establishes Rust's Camp near mouth of Bright Angel Creek. Theodore Roosevelt visits Grand Canyon. Sanger, King and E.B. (Hum) Wooley run from Lees Ferry to Yuma. Ralph Cameron charges a toll on Bright Angel Trail of $1/person until 1920.[8,110,137,169]
1904	Morning Star Mine (Mile 65R) in operation.[21,137]
1906	Theodore Roosevelt declares North Rim a National Game Preserve.[137]
1907	Russell and Monet expedition through GC. Rust builds cable car across river near Bright Angel Creek.[169]
1908	Theodore Roosevelt declares Grand Canyon a national monument.[137]

1910	Charles Spencer attempts to extract gold from Chinle Shale at Lees Ferry, bringing in a 92-ft stern wheeler "The Charles Spencer" to supply coal to the sluicing operation. The boat fails on its first upriver run due to strong currents. Spencer abandons the mining effort in 1912. The steamboat boiler is still visible at low water upstream from the launch ramp, and a hydraulic sluice pump sits on the upper terrace. In his 90s, Spencer returns to his mining claim at Paria in the 1960s to (unsuccessfully) mine rhenium.[21,137,242]
1911	Emery and Ellsworth Kolb run a single-boat trip through GC, ending in 1912. With the proceeds of the movie made on that trip, they build a popular tourist studio on the rim, which Emery runs until his death in 1976. A mysterious skeleton with a hole in the skull was found in a skiff in Emery's garage attic.[7,8,137,162,167,169]
1912	First automobile reaches Diamond Creek.[137]
1913	Kaibab Paiute Indian Reservation is established.
1914	Hermit's Rest tent camp hotel is built by Fred Harvey Co. in Hermit Canyon, and supplied by an improved trail and a 3000' cable car.[7,8,137]
1915	Russell, Tadje and Clement lose boat and end Grand Canyon filming trip at Slate Creek. John Waltenberg hauls their boat, "The Ross Wheeler" (constructed by, but stolen from Bert Loper) above the high water line at Upper Bass.[169]
1919	Grand Canyon is declared a National Park.[8,137]
1921	Rust's cablecar at Bright Angel Creek is replaced by a swinging bridge.[137]
1922	Fred Harvey Co. hires Mary Jane Colter to design "Phantom Ranch," which is constructed that year.[8,137]
1923	Claude Birdseye and EC La Rue, with Emery Kolb as head boatman. The crew runs the US Geological Survey mapping expedition through GC. La Rue's 1925 report set forth a plan for a stair-step of dams and reservoirs through the Colorado River's course.[27,165,166,167]
1927	Clyde Eddy makes two runs.[75,169]
1928	Lees Ferry discontinued after 3 die in a ferry mishap. The Kaibab (Black) Bridge is completed, with all cables and bridge parts carried by hand to Phantom Ranch.[69a,238,24]
1929	Navajo Bridge is completed, spanning the Colorado River at Marble Canyon. Glen and Bessie Hyde, "The Honeymoon Couple" run a sweep scow, but disappear. Their boat is found below Mile 232, where they likely perished.[137,242]
1932	The Western Canyon is declared a national monument. Desert View Watchtower (designed by Mary Jane Colter) is completed. Its ownership was turned over to the NPS in 2014.

National Park Service

Architect Mary Jane Colter began working for the Fred Harvey Company in 1910. For the next thirty years, she was one of few female architects. Colter completed 21 projects for Fred Harvey throughout the Southwest, including the 1922 Phantom Ranch buildings at the bottom of the Grand Canyon, and five structures on the South Rim: the Hopi House (1905), Hermit's Rest (1914), the observatory Lookout Studio (1914), Desert View Watchtower (1932), and the Bright Angel Lodge (1935). Colter decorated, but did not design, the El Tovar Hotel.

Bernard and Genevieve de Colmont and Antoine de Seynes ran self-supported in wooden frame, canvas skinned kayaks, 900 miles down the Green and Colorado Rivers in the fall of 1938, but were stopped at Lees Ferry by ice.

Mariott Library, University of Utah

The pre-commercial river trip era was dangerous, with a 5.2% chance of death.[21, 69b,169]

Beginning with the commercial era in 1938, the risk of death on the river decreased to 0.008% through 1999.

1934	The Civilian Conservation Corps established Camp 818 at the site of the present-day Phantom Ranch Campground to work on GC trails, bridges, and cross-canyon telephone line into 1936.[8,211]
1937	H. "Buzz" Holmstrom makes first solo trip through GC. Carnegie Institute expedition. A total of 192 people have passed some or all the way through Grand Canyon on the Colorado River.
1938	Norm Nevills' trip with Elzada Clover and Lois Jotter (the first women to go through GC) ushers in the commercial river running era. Amos Burg runs first inflatable boat through GC.[50,211,212a]
1941	Alex "Zee" Grant runs his kayak "Escalante" through with Nevills.[169]
1945–1946	Georgie Clark and Harry Aleson swim lower GC.[49]
1948	Hudson, "Dock" Marston, and Taylor quit motorized up-run attempt at Mile 217.[169]
1949	Hudson and Marston make first motorized down-run in the "Esmeralda II." Nevills and wife Doris die in a small plane crash.[137, 169,212a]
1950	Belknap Expedition. Marston motors through again.[169]
1951	Bob and Jim Rigg row through in 2 1/2 days. Jordan and Sanderson try outboard motors.
1954	Georgie Clark pioneers use of large, pontoon "G-rig."[4]
1955	Daggett and Beer swim from Lees Ferry to Lake Mead.
1956	Colorado River Storage Project Act approved, authorizing construction of Upper Basin dams. TWA and United Airlines crash over Chuar Butte near mouth of Little Colorado River kills 128.[8,137,181] Native "trash" fish in the upper Colorado River are poisoned to allow post-dam introduction of trout.
1960	Hamilton, Marston and others make only legal motorized uprun from Lake Mead to Lees Ferry.[169]
1963	Glen Canyon Dam completed. Marston runs 7 ft-long, one-man Sportyak through GC.[169,181]
1964	Glen Canyon Dam begins hydropower production.[181]
1965	Reclamation runs 65,000 cfs pulse flows to flush sand from Glen Canyon.[279,295-296]
1967	Robert Kennedy, George Plimpton, and Jim Whittaker run the river.[290]
1968	Rail service to South Rim discontinued due to easy automobile access.[290]
1969	Marble Canyon is declared a National Monument. Lost Orphan Mine on South Rim is closed.[8,21]
1970	Bright Angel (Silver) Bridge built, carrying Roaring Springs water to Indian Garden and South Rim.[8]
1973	Great increase in the number of river runners forces NPS to freeze private and commercial trip use. Twenty-two river companies run river trips.[8]

1975	Grand Canyon National Park and Havasupai Indian Reservation both enlarged.[8]
1976	More than 3 million visitors at Rims in one year.[8] Emery Kolb passes away.
1980	Lake Powell reservoir fills for first time.[279]
1982	Rewinding controversy and proposed increase in flow fluctuations provokes public outcry. Secretary of the Interior James Watt directs Reclamation to study dam effects, initiating Glen Canyon Environmental Studies Program, led by David L. Wegner.[299]
1983	Verlen Kruger and Steve Landick complete first non-motorized canoe up-run run through Grand Canyon in 21 days, portaging the larger rapids. They paddle up to Glen Canyon Dam in April-May, and carry their canoes through the dam tunnel into Lake Powell. Record inflow into a full Lake Powell reservoir causes spillway releases and flow to 92,600 cfs. Damage to dam exceeds $20 million. Kenton Grua, Rudi Petschek, and Steve Reynolds set non-motorized speed run through GC in a dory.[93,97a, 302]
1986	Airline Overflight Act passed, limiting air traffic routes.
1989	Secretary of the Interior Lujan calls for an *ex post facto* Environmental Impact Statement (EIS) on the operations of Glen Canyon Dam. Max and Thelma Biegert reopen Grand Canyon Railway from Williams to South Rim.[290,308]
1995	Glen Canyon Dam EIS completed, the nation's second largest at the time. It calls for reduced flow fluctuation, reduced ramping rates, experimental floods, and an adaptive management program (AMP).[308]
1996	First planned flood of 45,000 conducted for 7 days in in April-March to test use of high flows for sediment management.[221,308,328] Record of Decision on the operations of Glen Canyon Dam approved by Secretary of the Interior.
1997	AMP initiated with formation of Adaptive Management Work Group as a Federal Advisory Committee, served by a Technical Work Group and provided with information by the USGS Grand Canyon Monitoring and Research Center. Budget $11 million/yr.[274]
2000	Test of steady flows during summer fails to improve conditions for native fish and riparian vegetation.[235]
2006	NPS finalizes Colorado River Management Plan on river running recreation in Grand Canyon.[304]
2012	Secretary Salazar approves AMWG Desired Future Conditions for the Colorado River ecosystem. High flow experiments in 2004, 2008, 2012–2014, and 2016 used to study and manage sediment mass balance, resulting in Secretarial acceptance of high flows criteria.[303,309]
2016	Long Term Experimental Management Plan EIS approved, assuring continued adaptive management.

Grand Canyon Railway engines 4960 and 29 at the Grand Canyon depot, 2005.

Drew Jacksich

Conservation History of Grand Canyon by Kim Crumbo and Larry Stevens

Subjugation of most southwestern Native American Tribes by the US Government in the 1870s–1880s opened the doors to settlement and rapid exploitation of the region's natural resources.[209] The extreme winter of 1886–1887 resulted in a major die-off of western cattle and, in a twist of fate, that winter's cattle losses encouraged Theodore Roosevelt to turn from cattle ranching in North Dakota back into politics.[30] Benjamin Harrison, then a Senator, had introduced three unsuccessful Grand Canyon National Park bills between 1882 and 1886. President Benjamin Harrison established the Grand Canyon Forest Reserve in 1893, prompted by on-going degradation of natural values of the Grand Canyon region.

In 1903 Theodore Roosevelt visited the Canyon and famously declared: "The Grand Canyon fills me with awe. It is beyond comparison—beyond description; absolutely unparalleled throughout the wide world... Let this great wonder of nature remain as it now is. Do nothing to mar its grandeur, sublimity and loveliness. You cannot improve on it. But what you can do is to keep it for your children, your children's children, and all who come after you, as the one great sight... every American should see."[137] Roosevelt did much to protect Grand Canyon, but he could scarcely foresee the struggles that lay ahead to preserve this great American treasure.

By 1905, Congress and President Theodore Roosevelt recognized that forests like those on the Kaibab Plateau should also be set aside "for the wild forest creatures...[to] afford perpetual protection to the native fauna and flora." In 1906, and in accordance with earlier Congressional authorization, Roosevelt established the Grand Canyon National Game Preserve for "the protection of game animals... recognized as a breeding place therefore..." That designation, while still on the books, has proven ineffective in preserving the full array of native species and their habitats, especially large carnivores, as well as the Kaibab Plateau's old growth forests and grasslands. Exasperated by faint-hearted Congressional reluctance to protect Grand Canyon, Roosevelt used his 1906 Antiquities Act to proclaim the area a National Monument in 1908, laying the foundation for National Park status, but lexcluding most of the forested Kaibab Plateau.[209]

Early efforts to protect the lands surrounding Grand Canyon continued with recommendations to enlarge the monument to five million ac (2 million ha) by including the North Kaibab and Tusayan Ranger Districts and a portion of Utah's Dixie National Forest. Two decades after Roosevelt's Game Preserve designation, "Ding" Darling, Director of the U.S. Biological Survey, proposed creating a vast wildlife area on the Arizona Strip (in Arizona lying north of the Colorado River). At least one rancher, Preston Nutter, expressed enthusiasm for the idea.[231] However, other ranchers and loggers in the area opposed Darling's proposal and defeated the measure.[209] On 26 February 1919, just three months after the end of World War I, President Woodrow Wilson established Grand Canyon National Park. The enabling legislation continued to be modified until at least 1925 to account for water development projects on the Colorado River. In 1927, Congress enlarged the Park to include southern portions of the North Kaibab forest.[137] In December 1932 President Herbert Hoover established a 273,145 ac Grand Canyon National Monument in the Toroweap area west of the Park.[209,231] Opposition by ranchers and loggers to closure of these lands continued through the 1930s.

With the passage of the 1956 Colorado River Storage Project Act, giving states of the Upper Basin leverage against California (see Chapter 6), and the building of Glen Canyon Dam, other dams were planned and promoted in Grand Canyon. Marble Canyon Dam, sited for construction just below Red Wall Cavern at Mile 39.5, would have inundated 53 mi (85 km) of the river corridor, up to near the base of Glen Canyon Dam. Marble Canyon Dam would have eliminated one of the world's most enchanting river canyons. Also proposed, Bridge Canyon Dam was to be constructed at Mile 236 and would have flooded 95 miles of the lower Canyon, including Lava Falls and lower Havasu Creek.

As late as 1966, many considered these dams inevitable, but in June of that year and putting his job on the line, then Director of the Sierra Club, David Brower launched an all-out public campaign to save Grand Canyon from Marble Canyon Dam. The Sierra Club's full-page advertisements in the New York Times and Washington Post read: "Only You Can Save the Grand Canyon from being Flooded—For Profit" and "Should we also flood the Sistine Chapel so tourists can get nearer the ceiling?"[27,55] In 1968, after much debate and political maneuvering, Congress passed and President Lyndon Johnson signed Public Law 90-537, prohibiting the study or construction of hydroelectric dams in Grand Canyon without congressional approval. On

January 20, 1969, his last day in office, President Johnson created Marble Canyon National Monument.[130] In 1975, President Ford signed the Grand Canyon National Park Enlargement Act, combining Marble and Grand Canyon National Monuments into a much larger Grand Canyon National Park, protecting most of the Canyon from Lees Ferry to the Grand Wash Cliffs, and expanding the Havasupai Indian Reservation to include traditional Tribal lands on the South Rim.[8]

Subsequent to the enlargement of the Park, regional conservation groups began working to restore native species and natural ecosystems in the region. Recognizing the historical context and the importance of preservation of large tracts of Grand Canyon's watershed, efforts to protect the Canyon renewed. Grand Canyon Wildlands Council, Grand Canyon Trust, Sierra Club and other conservation partners and supporters worked with former Interior Secretary Bruce Babbitt for protection of unprotected areas on the Arizona Strip. In 2000 President Clinton established the Grand Canyon-Parashant and Vermilion Cliffs National Monuments. Collectively, these two land units are larger than Grand Canyon National Park, and protect lower elevation portions of the North Rim watershed.

During the first session of the 112th Congress, Representative Raul Grijalva introduced legislation to protect Grand Canyon's watershed outside of the Park from additional uranium mining claims and subsequent mining impacts. Although that legislation failed (it was reintroduced in 2013), public insistence in 2012 resulted in the Secretary of the Interior withdrawing from future mining 1 million acres surrounding Grand Canyon National Park. This temporary withdrawal order is to last for 20 yr, but Congress has been unwilling to provide long-term protection of the natural values critical to the region's economic and environmental welfare. The mining industry has filed at least four recent lawsuits seeking repeal of the withdrawal. Conservationists, led by Grand Canyon Wildlands and Wildlands Network remain committed to following Theodore Roosevelt's lead and fulfilling the vision to permanently protect Grand Canyon and its surrounding watershed on an ecologically complete scale, including regional wildlife corridors and the ancient forests of the Kaibab Plateau.

For updates on conservation issues go to GrandCanyon Wildlands.org.

V. BIOLOGY AND ECOLOGY

The Colorado River Ecosystem

Although in many places just a thin skein of microbial, spiderweb, or plant life clinging to cliff surfaces, the biology of the Colorado River ecosystem (CRE) in lower Glen and Grand Canyons is as rich and varied as its geology and human history. More than 12,000 macroscopic species are likely to occur within about 500 vertical feet (150 m) of the river in Grand Canyon,[39, 46, 121, 133, 185, 259, 289] including nearly 800 of the Canyon's 1,800 plant species, nearly 400 vertebrate species, and perhaps 10,000 macroinvertebrate species (round and segmented worms, mollusks, and arthropods). About 2,500 invertebrate species have been documented thus far. Native plants and animals in the Canyon provide insight into how life persists in these harsh landscapes, and how biogeography and evolution are affected by this large, deep canyon landscape.[270] Many non-native species also exist in the river corridor, including salt ceder (*Tamarix* spp.), camelthorn (*Alhagi maurorum*), cheatgrasses (*Bromus* spp.) and nearly 200 other introduced plant species, as well as 20 fish species, several birds and mammals, a few terrestrial insects, the shrimp-like *Gammarus* scud,[271] Louisiana red crayfish (*Procambarus clarkii*; so far only below Mile 245), and New Zealand mudsnails (*Potamopyrgus antipodarum*). Invasive quagga mussels (*Dreissena rostriformis bugensis*) are rapidly colonizing the region, with potentially dire consequences for the CRE. In this chapter, we'll delve into the Canyon's rich biodiversity, and the structure and distribution of assemblages there, across steep ecological gradients of time, space, productivity, and disturbance that limit life's expression in this arid river ecosystem.

"(T)he Grand Cañon of the Colorado, the most stupendous chasm known, is a gigantic illustration of ... the cutting power of water and the carving power of sand; while the terrific thunder-storms and cloud-bursts ... shake the very foundations of the earth in their fury, shattering tall pines with the(ir) lightning, and sending mighty torrents down the hillsides to plow deep gorges in the desert, serve to indicate the resistless energy of the forces of the air."

C. Hart Merriam 1890:29

Quagga Mussel
Non-native Quagga Mussel (*Dreissen rostriformis bugensis*) represent an enormous threat to the Colorado River ecosystem. Shown actual size.

Life Zones of the Grand Canyon Region.[202]

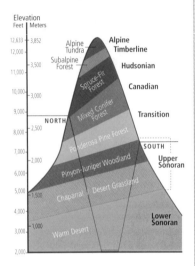

Figure 5.1
C. Hart Merriam's life zones are based on the distribution of vegetation across elevation. His 1890 biological survey of northern Arizona from the top of the San Francisco Peaks to the bottom of Grand Canyon was the first study of its kind in North America.

A Grand Ecotone

Plant species and vegetation structure is used to describe ecosystems, and part of what contributes to the great biodiversity of the Grand Canyon ecoregion is that it is a grand *ecotone,* a mixing zone of several *biomes* (suites of related ecosystems)[270] The Great Basin, Sonoran, and Mohave Deserts all converge in the region, along with Maderan (Mexican), Rocky Mountain, and Intermountain biomes. Over the past 13,000 yr the region's vegetation has come to its present state. We generally think of plants as only gradually shifting their distributions in response to changing climate regimes; however, colonization rates can be surprisingly fast. For example, Pinyon Jays (*Gymnorhinus cyanocephalus*) disperse pinyon pine nuts, and likely are responsible for the rapid post-Pleistocene spread of pinyon pine (*Pinus edulis* and *P. monophylla*) throughout the Southwest.

Today the vegetation of the Grand Canyon region includes cold-adapted, dry-summer **Great Basin Desert** plant species that are typical of Nevada and western Utah, such as bigtooth sagebrush (*Artemesia tridentata*) and roundleaf buffalo-berry (*Shepherdia rotundifolia*).[270] The appearance of bean-family catclaw (*Acacia greggii*) and mesquite (*Prosopis glandulosa* var. *torreyana*) shrubby trees at Mile 39 signals the furthest upstream and northern-most extension of these plants from the **Sonoran Desert**—the hot, wet-summer desert of central and southern Arizona and northwestern Mexico. Other plants that are characteristic of the Sonora Desert include brittlebush (*Encelia farinosa*), prickly pears (*Opuntia* spp.) and various low-growing cacti. To the west of Grand Canyon, the **Mohave Desert** is the hot, dry-summer desert of Lake Mead that supports creosote-bush (*Larrea tridentata)*, which occurs upriver to Mile 169L, as well as Mohave yucca (*Yucca mohavensis*) and the scarecrow-like Joshua tree (*Yucca brevifolia*). However, neither of those yucca species occur in Grand Canyon. The **Maderan Biome** lies immediately south of the Colorado Plateau, and supports neotropical and Mexican species that occur farther south. That flora advanced northward during the most recernt post-glacial phase. Grand Canyon winters are too cold for saguaro cactus (*Carnegiea gigantea*), the characteristic Maderan columnar cactus of the Sonoran Desert in central and southern Arizona. The **Intermountain and Rocky Mountain Biomes** are boreal tundra, coniferous forest and woodland habitats that moved downslope and southward during glacial times, but which have retreated upslope and northward during warm interglacial period.

In addition to regional mixing of the biota within biomes, elevation strongly affects climate and plant distributions; a subject first studied in the U.S. by Merriam in 1890. (Fig. 5.1)[202] **Lower Sonoran Zone** creosote-bush desert shrub vegetation grows up to nearly 4,000 ft (1,200 m) elevation, **Upper Sonoran Zone** pinyon-juniper occurs from 4000-6000+ ft (1,200-1,850m), **Transition Zone** ponderosa pine-Gambel's oak forest grows from 6000-8000+ ft (1,850-2,450 m) elevation, **Canadian Zone** Douglas and white fir occur from 8,000-9,500 ft (2,450-2900 m), and the **Hudsonian Zone** spruce-fir forest occurs from 8,500-11,000 ft (2,600-3,350 m) elevation. Although no high-elevation **Alpine Tundra** habitat exists in Grand Canyon National Park, a small amount of this habitat is found above 11,500 ft (3,505 m) elevation on the top of the San Francisco Peaks just south of the Park.

Biogeography in the World's Most Famous Large, Deep Canyon

As a large, deep canyon, Grand Canyon influences the distribution of more than 75% of the plant and animal species that live in and around it in three important ways: as a barrier/filter, a corridor, or a refuge.[270] The chasm functions as an obvious across-canyon barrier to movement, keeping endemic taxa such as the North Rim Kaibab squirrel (*Sciurus aberti kaibabensis*) from breeding with the South Rim tassel-eared squirrel (*S. a. aberti*), and the endemic South Rim Grand Canyon ringlet butterfly (*Coenomorpha tullia*

National Park Service

California Condor

In Pleistocene times the California Condor (*Gymnogyps californianus*) soared across the southern United States, and their bones show up in Grand Canyon caves.[79] California Condors have the largest wingspan of any North American terrestrial bird (9.8 ft, 3.0 m), and easily fly 100 mi (160 km) per day, searching for animal carcasses on which they scavenge. Loss of large ungulate prey and predator poisoning programs since the 1880s led to the precipitous decline of this species.[256] A successful breeding and release program by the U.S. Fish and Wildlife Service and the Peregrine Fund (www.peregrinefund.org) since 1996 has resulted in 75 of these big scavenging birds soaring through the Grand Canyon region, with several successful nesting attempts; however, they are still highly susceptible to lead poisoning from hunter-shot carcasses.

furcae) from reaching the North Rim.[98] But the Canyon also serves as an upstream-downstream barrier. Some species, such as the desert horned lizard (*Phrynosoma platyrhinos* and *P. Hernandesi*) and rabbits occur widely on the rims and both upstream and downstream from Grand Canyon, but do not occur in the river corridor due to environmental or habitat limitations. Kangaroo rats (*Dipodomys* spp.) also are oddly absent from the river corridor, and termites are anomalously uncommon.[270]

In an opposite fashion, the Canyon serves as a riparian corridor through harsh desert terrain, providing habitat and an avenue of movement, migration, or wash-through for many desert species, from or into the Upper Colorado River Basin. Fish, many species of birds and bats, monarch butterflies, and mobile species move or migrate through the river corridor. Although its path is now blocked by dams, the huge, predatory, highly mobile Colorado Pikeminnow (*Ptychocheilus lucius*; 6 ft long – 1.8 m, and weighing up to 100 pounds – 45 kg)[145, 311] may have engaged in long-distance spawning runs through Grand Canyon and into the upper Colorado River basin. In addition to migrants, many desert biota occupy the thin strip of desert-riparian habitat on the floor of Grand Canyon, which is surrounded by cold, high elevation plateau lands. Among these desert dwellers are: honey mesquite, catclaw accacia, and many other desert plant species; numerous aquatic insects; Rocky Mountain and Red-spotted Toads (*Anaxyrus woodhousii* and *A. punctatus,* respectively); two collared lizard species (*Crotaphytus* spp.) and other reptiles; rodents (Beaver – *Castor canadensis*, and pocket and deer mice), and other mammals. Floods disperse plant propagules downstream, and some of these upper elevation species germinate and become established along the river but may not be able to reproduce.[1] Such "waif" species include the following: Apache Plume (*Fallugia paradoxa*) reaches its lowest elevation limit at Mile 14L, Dune Broom (*Parryella filifolia)* occurs in only 3 localities in the upper half of the CRE; Poison Ivy (*Toxicodendron rydbergii*) only occurs along the river at Vaseys Paradise (Mile 32R), Lower Deer Creek Spring (Mile 136R), and Mile 142R Spring; and Shrub Snowberry (*Symphoricarpos oreophilus*) only occurs along the river down to about Mile 2L.[270]

As a refuge the Canyon harbors rare and endemic forms, such as McDougall's Flaveria sunflowers and Aaron-Ross's Spurge (*Euphorbia aaron-rossii*). In addition to plants, the Masked Clubskimmer dragonfly

A remarkable place to see the influences of aspect on Canyon vegetation is at the Anasazi Bridge (Mile 43.5), in one of the deepest incised river meanders in the world. Looking downstream towards Point Hansbrough, river right is a north-facing slope that supports desert grassland, Mormon tea, and an occasional juniper, hackberry, and buffalo-berry shrub. In contrast, the desert slopes on river left support Sonoran Desert brittlebush, catclaw, and cacti, and virtually no grass. East- and west-facing slopes in this reach support a mix of species from north- and south-facing slopes, and therefore have greater species richness. What makes the aspect story even more compelling there is that just a mile downstream, around the bend of the Point Hansbrough meander, aspect is reversed and the vegetation largely follows suit. Other segments of the river where aspect effects are obvious include Miles 120-123, Mile 142, and Miles 197-199.

River Corridor Habitats and Plant Species

Overview: Different kinds of habitats support different plant assemblages in the river corridor and in the lower reaches of tributaries.[47, 225] Talus-slope associations consist of xeric-adapted (desert) species (Plate 5A). Mesic-adapted (moisture-loving) communities occur at the river's edge and in protected side-canyons. Riparian (streamside) vegetation stands out in sharp contrast to the harsh, pristine desert above the predam 10-yr flood line at about 130,000 cfs (3,861 m³/s) stage.[47, 149, 225, 297] These plant associations change as one proceeds downriver and descends in elevation, responding to the gradients mentioned above, temperature regime (especially the length of freezing periods), and disturbance (i.e., inundation, rockfall, etc.). Canyon wildflowers respond strongly to seasonal precipitation patterns, blooming in profusion after wet winters that have at least one good storm each month from November through March (Plate 5B).[138]

Inner Canyon Fauna

Overview: Due to its position as a mixing zone between the Mexican Maderan and the boreal biomes, the Canyon shares faunal affinities with the deserts to the west and south of the Colorado Plateau, as well as with the Intermountain West and Rocky Mountains to the north and east. Although often nocturnal and difficult to see, animal life in the Canyon is diverse and well worth the effort of observation.[36, 98, 133, 168, 205] Checklists for the vertebrates of the park are available online or from the Grand Canyon Association. The species described below include only those commonly detected in the river corridor or a short distance up tributaries.

Common Invertebrates: The river corridor supports a vast array of insect and other arthropod life (Plate 5D). Tarantulas are common but rarely seen in the Canyon and are relatively harmless. Black-widow spiders (*Latrodectus* spp.) are common in cliff faces and crevices, but are shy, sedentary, and nocturnal. Kaibab Recluse Spiders (*Loxosceles kaiba*) are abundant in Canyon caves and rockshelters, but also are timid. The most common Canyon

Talus-Slope Vegetation: Shadscale (*Atriplex confertifolia*), Mormon tea (*Ephedra* spp.), hedgehog and prickly pear cacti, the clustered Barrel Cactus–like Cottontop Cactus (*Echinocactus polycephalus*), Narrow-leaf Yucca (*Yucca baileyi*), and Utah Century Plant (*Agave utahensis*) are common talus-slope plants in the upper Canyon (Plate 5C). Note that upstream from Mile 100, Utah Century Plants grow as single rosettes for a decade or two, then bloom spectacularly and die; however, downstream from Mile 100, from river to rim, this same species of century plant makes "pups"— vegetative offshoots that can grow, bloom, and die while attached to the mother plant. Therefore, the genetic individual plant lives much longer than those upstream. Perhaps this transition is due to the harshness of the western Canyon, or perhaps it is due to ancient human intervention in the population of this much-harvested species.

Below Mile 40 and into the middle of the Canyon, many other talus plant species appear, including Brittlebush (*Encelia farinosa*), Alkali Jimmyweed (*Isocoma acredenia*), and true Barrel Cactus (*Ferocactus cylindraceus*—look for the latter downstream from Mile 110). Creosote-bush (*Larrea tridentata*), ocotillo, chollas, Whipple Yucca, and Crucifixion-thorn (*Canotia holacantha*) occur on the talus slope community in the lower Canyon. Both on north-facing desert slopes and along the river, Red Brome (*Bromus rubens*) and other non-native grasses and herbs turn Canyon slopes green in March and April, but increase the risk of summertime fire in a landscape where wildfire is naturally rare.

Riverside Plant Assemblages: Along the river, several distinctive parallel bands of vegetation grow at different elevations above the river.[47, 225, 279] Below the xeric desert vegetation, but above the 10-yr predam flood stage is the upper riparian zone. It is characterized by (in upper Marble Canyon) Apache Plume (*Fallugia paradoxa*), and below Mile 39 by Honey Mesquite and Catclaw. Four-wing Saltbush, Fremont Pepperweed (*Lepidium fremontii*), Netleaf Hackberry (*Celtis laevis reticulata*—which grows along the river between the pre-dam 3–5 yr return flood stage), and California Redbud shrubs (*Cercis occidentalis*) also occur in this zone. Just downslope, and flooded on a 2-10 year basis in post-dam time is the middle riparian zone. Largely devoid of vegetation in pre-dam time, it is now co-dominated by desert and riparian species, including Brittlebush, Snakeweed (*Gutierrezia sarothrae*) and, in the lower Canyon, by Desert Broom (*Baccharis sarothroides*).

A verdant belt of perennial plant species grows in the lower riparian zone, which was annually scoured by predam floods, but is now inundated occasionally and briefly by planned floods. The plant species that occupy that zone are phreatophytes, whose roots reach the water table. Formerly the most conspicu-

scorpion is the straw-colored Bark Scorpion *(Centruroides sculpturatus)*, which packs a very serious sting. In contrast, the larger, more formidable-looking Arizona Giant Hairy Scorpion *(Hadrurus spadix)* has a far less toxic sting. Scorpions are strictly nocturnal, but make sure to shake out your shoes and life jacket before putting them on in the morning, particularly in August when the young are dispersing. Scorpions' preferred habitat is beneath driftwood or rocks, but they also move through riverside vegetation at night. Red harvester ants *(Pogonomyrmex*, especially *P. californicus)* are abundant on beaches and trails, and sting with a vengeance. Their venom is one of the most toxic known, but fortunately it is delivered only in minute quantities. House, bluebottle,

ous species there was hybrid Tamarisk or Salt-cedar (*Tamarix chinensis* x *ramosissima*). Introduced after 1900, tamarisk quickly spread through the Colorado River basin because of its enormous production of small, windblown seeds and vigorous growth.[210] However, the release of the Tamarisk Leaf Beetle (*Diorhabda carinulata*) dooms the continued dominance of salt-cedar in the river corridor. Native phreatophytes that have colonized the lower riparian zone include horsetail (*Equisetum ferrisii*), Coyote Willow (*Salix exigua*), Honey Mesquite, three species of seep-willows (*Baccharis* spp.), Common Reed (*Phragmites australis*), and numerous non-native grasses and herbs. Downstream from Havasu Canyon, non-native Bermuda-grass (*Cynodon dactylon*) strongly dominates mesic lower riparian terraces.[199] A few remaining Goodding's Willow trees (*Salix gooddingii*) occur along the river, but may soon disappear from the corridor due to beaver depredation. At and sometimes just below the river's edge is the hydro-riparian zone, a frequently flooded habitat that is dominated by fluvial marsh species, such as horsetail, Common Reed, Cattail (*Typha domingensis*), Water-sedge (*Carex emoryi*) and rushes (e.g. *Juncus balticus* and *J. articulatus*).

Side Canyon Vegetation:[138, 225] Tributaries of the Colorado River are often cooler and more mesic than the mainstream corridor. These conditions promote the growth of different shrub and tree species. At Vaseys Paradise (Mile 32R) Redbud, Poison Ivy, and Coyote Willow predominate over lush beds of maidenhair fern (*Adiantum capillus-veneris*), April-blooming Heleborine Orchid (*Epipactis gigantea*), Cardinal Monkey-flower (*Mimulus cardinalis*), and Watercress (*Nasturtium officinale*). A rare yellow form of Cardinal Monkey-flower grows on the upstream side of the main pourout. John Wesley Powell named this springs complex for botanist George W. Vasey who traveled with him in the West prior to his 1869 river trip.[137] In Saddle Canyon, a box canyon at Mile 47.5R, numerous Catclaw, redbud, and hackberry trees grow near the entrance, while Hop-tree (*Ptelea trifoliata* var. *pallida*), a formidable stand of the holly-like Fremont Barberry (*Berberis fremontii*), and Box Elder trees (*Acer negundo*) occur towards the back. A regionally endemic giant thistle (*Cirsium rydbergii*) is common along the creek, also occurring in Buck Farm Canyon (Mile 41R). Fremont Cottonwood trees (*Populus fremontii*) are seen in many of the larger side canyons, but saplings rarely escape hungry beaver along the mainstream. Arizona Wild Grape (*Vitis arizonica*) is rare along the river but grows profusely along Havasu Creek (Mile 157L) and elsewhere. Three small populations of a newly described century plant (*Agave phillipsiana*) occur in several tributaries in the middle of Grand Canyon.[131a] These may have been brought into Grand Canyon by the Pueblo Indians.

Tarantula Hawk

More than 1000 bee, ant and wasp species occur in the Grand Canyon ecoregion. The largest Canyon wasps (Plate 5D) are the orange or black-winged tarantula hawks (*Pepsis grossus* and *Hemipepsis ustulata*), which seek out and do battle with tarantulas. After subduing and paralyzing her quarry, a female tarantula hawk lays an egg on the spider and buries it. The larva eats the parylized, but still living, spider one leg at a time.

Velvet Ant

Velvet ants (Mutillidae; Plate 5D) are one of the many interesting wasps found in the Canyon. Hard-stinging and white to brightly colored, the wingless females parasitize the larvae of ground-nesting bees. Female *Dasymutilla gloriosa*, a small white species commonly seen in the lower Canyon, resembles a creosotebush seed. Male velvet ants are brightly colored and winged, but harmless.

and flesh flies are harmless but bothersome pests, particularly during the spring and fall months. Mosquitoes are generally rare[284] but Stable Flies (*Stomoxys calcitrans*), Buffalo Gnats (*Simiuliium arcticum*), and, near Diamond Creek in the spring months, "nosee-ums" (*Leptoconops* spp.) are biting flies that can be quite annoying.

The most conspicuous springtime butterflies are the Mourning Cloak (*Nymphalis antiopa*), various whites (*Pontia* spp.), and the brick-and-black Acastus Patch (*Chlosyne acastus*), but more than 140 other species occur in or near Grand Canyon.[98] Among the more striking summer butterflies are the Many-tailed Swallowtail (*Papilio multicaudata*–Arizona's state butterfly), Queen (*Danaus gilippus*), Monarch (*Danaus plexippus*), and Arizona Sister (*Adelpha eulalia*).

Aquatic insects abound in many Grand Canyon tributaries (Plate 5D).[218a] Dragonfly and damselfly larvae are abundant in many Grand Canyon waters, sitting and waiting for soft-bodied aquatic prey. Dragonflies rest with their wings outstretched, while damselflies are often smaller and fold their wings at rest.[273] The Flame Skimmer Dragonfly (*Libellula saturata*) and the small blue Vivid Dancer Damselfly (*Argia vivida*) are the most common of the 58 Odonata species in Grand Canyon. Spring-fed streams from Nankoweap down to Stone Creek support the only breeding population of Masked Club Skimmer Dragonflies (*Brechmorhoga pertinax*) in the U.S.[272] Water striders (*Aquarius remigis*) and tiny *Microvelia* water bugs ply the surfaces of quiet side canyon pools, such as those in Elves Chasm (Mile 116.5L).[277] Backswimmers (*Notonecta lobata*) hang upside in those pools, and yellow-flecked predaceous diving beetles (*Thermonectus marmoratus*) and blue-green water scavenger beetles (*Hydrochara lineata*) prowl the depths. On the bottom of the pools case-dragging caddisflies labor through the ooze, while mayfly larvae scurry about. In the cooler, swifter Canyon tributaries, stonefly nymphs cling to the undersides of rocks, but scuttle away when predatory hellgrammites (*Corydalus texa-*

nus) appear. Hellgrammites are the the Loch Ness Monsters of the aquatic insect world, but are distantly related to lacewings and the tiny ant lions that dig conical pits and furrow-like tracks in dry sand in protected areas.

Before 1963 the Colorado River was likely too sediment-laden and too turbulent to support abundant invertebrate life, and the clear, cold river has been slow to attract invertebrates.[135, 282, 288] Earthworms and larval buffalo gnats and midges (Chironomidae) live in bottom sediments or in macrophytic vegetation, feeding on diatoms and filamentous green algae.[58, 281] The shrimp-like amphipod scud, *Gammarus lacustris*, is common in the upper Canyon and was introduced as food for trout.[281, 287] Nonnative New Zealand Mudsnail (*Potamopyrgus antipodarum*) widely colonized the river after 1995, but a potentially much greater threat to the river ecosystem is the impending invasion of the Quagga Mussel (*Dreissena rostriformis bugensis*). Quagga Mussels are now common in Lake Mead, costing $1 million/year to control. As of 2017 we found densities at Lees Ferry of 1,000/m^2.

Fish: Prior to 1880, eight species of native fish were found in the lower Colorado River, including those listed in Table 5.1[206] Five of those eight native fish species are endemic, occurring in no other river basin (Plate 5E).

Table 5.1
Fish Species of the Colorado River in Lower Glen Canyon and Grand Canyon

NATIVE FISH		INTRODUCED FISH			
Bonytail Chub (*Gila elegans*)	E	Rainbow Trout (*Oncorhynchus mykiss*)	A	Channel Catfish (*Ictalurus punctatus*)	N
Humpback Chub (*Gila cypha*)	C-N	Cutthroat Trout (*Oncorhynchus clarkii*)	R	Black Bullhead (*Ameiurus melas*)	A
Roundtail Chub (*Gila robusta*)	E	Brown Trout (*Salmo trutta*)	N	Rio Grande Killifish (*Fundulus zebrinus*)	C
Colorado Pikeminnow (*Ptychocheilus lucius*)	E	Brook Trout (*Salvelinus fontinalis*)	R	Striped Bass (*Morone saxatalis*)	N
Speckled Dace (*Rhinichthys osculus*)	A	Common Carp (*Cyprinus c. carpio*)	A	Largemouth Bass (*Micropterus salmoides*)	N
Paria River Dace (*Rhinichthys osculus* ssp.)	R	Goldfish (*Carassius auratus*)	R	Smallmouth Bass (*Micropterus dolomieu*)	R
Meriwhithica Dace (*Rhinichthys osculus* ssp.)	R	Fathead Minnow (*Pimephales promelas*)	R	Green Sunfish (*Lepomis cyanellus*)	R
Razorback Sucker (*Xyrauchen texanus*)	E-P	Guppy (*Poecilia reticulata*, Havasu Creek)	R	Bluegill Sunfish (*Lepomis macrochirus*)	R
Flannelmouth Sucker (*Catostomus latipinnis*)	A			Walleye (*Sander vitreus*)	R
Bluehead Sucker (*Catostomus discobolus*)	C				

KEY | **Abundance:** **A**-Abundant, **C**-Common, **E**-Extirpated, **N**-Uncommon, **P**-Population re-established, **R**-Rare.

With 64% of its fish species unique, the Colorado has the highest proportion of endemic fish of any US river basin. However, today only five native fish species remain: Humpback Chub; Flannelmouth, Bluehead and Razorback Suckers (*Catostomus* spp. and *Xyrauchen texanus*, respectively), and Speckled Dace (*Rhinichthys osculus*). The decline of native fish has been attributed to dam operations and the introduction of non-native fish (particularly brown trout – *Salmo trutta*) as well as 17 species of introduced fish parasites.[48, 206] The river and its tributaries presently support about 20 exotic fish species (Table 5.1) The stretch of river from Lees Ferry up to Glen Canyon Dam is regarded as one of the finest trophy trout fisheries in the Southwest. Nonnative catfish (Ictaluridae) and Common Carp (*Cyprinus carpio*) were well established in the lower Colorado River by 1914,[113] but like the voracious Striped Bass (*Morone saxatilis*), they prefer warmer waters. Striped Bass weighing nearly 70 pounds (32 kg) have been taken from lower Grand Canyon and Lake Mead.

The endangered Humpback Chub (*Gila cypha*) is an odd-shaped fish and is endemic to the Colorado River basin. The chub's pronounced dorsal hump reduces the likelihood of predation by Colorado Pikeminnow.[206, 227, 298, 310] Formerly widespread throughout the lowland portions of both Colorado River basins, and caught in abundance at Lees Ferry immediately after closure of Glen Canyon Dam, it has entirely disappeared from many reaches of the river. It is now restricted to four populations in the Upper Basin, a large breeding population around the mouth of the LCR, and in lower Grand Canyon.[50a, 313] Of the 10 Humpback Chub aggregations in Grand Canyon, only those at Mile 30, LCR, Havasu Creek, and lower Grand Canyon reproduce. Mainstream chub undertake a springtime spawning run from April-June into the lower LCR. They are opportunistic predators, feeding on aquatic and terrestrial invertebrates, and on smaller fish including their own young. Chub live 20 years or more. Reasons for its endangerment include dam-related colder water temperatures and the introduction of non-native piscivorous fish and fish parasites, but the current population (8,000+ fish) appears to be stable and recovering. Young chubs drifting from the LCR in summer enter the cold mainstream, which may shock them physiologically, retard their growth, and expose them to predatious non-native fish.

Amphibians and Reptiles:[29, 205] Six species of amphibians recently occurred in the river corridor, but two *Lithobates* leopard frog species were extirpated in post-dam time (Table 5.2; Plate 5F). Rocky Mountain Toads (*Anaxyrus woodhousii*) are generally more common along the mainstream in riparian habitats, while Red-

-spotted Toads (*Anaxyrus punctatus*) are generally dominant in tributary canyons. The sheep-like call of the Canyon Treefrog (*Hyla arenicolor*) is most often heard in tributary canyons, where they sit in shallow water or perch on smooth stone surfaces near water. Canyon Treefrogs readily change color to match their background. Tiger Salamanders (*Ambystoma mavortium*) were recently discovered in the river upstream from Lees Ferry.

Table 5.2
Amphibians and Reptiles of the Colorado River in Lower Glen Canyon and Grand Canyon

AMPHIBIANS

Rocky Mountain Toad (*Anaxyrus woodhousii*)	C	T
Red-spotted Toad (*Anaxyrus punctatus*)	C	T
Canyon Treefrog (*Hyla arenicolor*)	C	T
Northern Leopard Frog (*Lithobates pipiens*)	E	U
Relict? Leopard Frog (*Lithobates* nr. *onca*)	E	L
Tiger Salamander (*Ambystoma mavortium*)	R	LF

LIZARDS

Banded Gecko (*Coleonyx variegatus*)	C	T
Gila Monster (*Heloderma suspectum cinctum*)	R	L
Chuckwalla (*Sauromalus ater*)	C	T
Zebra-tailed Lizard (*Callisaurus draconoides*)	E,P,R	DC
Great Basin Collared Lizard (*Crotaphytus bicinctores*)	C	T
Eastern Collared Lizard (*Crotaphytus collaris*)	C	T
Leopard Lizard (*Gambelia wizlizenii*)	R	LF, DC
Yellow-backed Spiny Lizard (*Sceloporus magister*)	C	T
Side-blotched Lizard (*Uta stansburiana*)	A	T
Tree Lizard (*Urosaurus ornatus*)	C	T
Desert Horned Lizard (*Phrynosoma platyrhinos*)	R	LF, DC
Western Whiptail (*Aspidoscelis tigris*)	A	T

SNAKES

Western Threadsnake (*Leptotyphlops humilis*)	R	M
Ringneck Snake (*Diadophis punctatus*)	R	M,L
Coachwhip (*Masticophis flagellum*)	R	L
Striped Whip Snake (*Masticophis taeniatus*)	N	T
Western Patch-nosed Snake (*Salvadora hexalepis*)	N	T
Gopher Snake (*Pituophis catenifer*)	N	T
California Kingsnake (*Lampropeltis getulus*)	C	M,L
Long-nosed Snake (*Rhinocheilus lecontei*)	R	M,L
Sonoran Lyre Snake (*Trimorphodon biscutatus*)	R	U,M
Night Snake (*Hypsiglena torquata*)	R	M,L
Ground Snake (*Sonora semiannulata*)	R	M,L
Western Diamondback Rattlesnake (*Crotalus atrox*)	N	DC
Speckled Rattlesnake (*Crotalus mitchelli*)	C	L
Black-tailed Rattlesnake (*Crotalus molossus*)	N	L
Grand Canyon (pink) Rattlesnake (*Crotalus oreganus abyssus*)	C	U,M
Hopi Rattlesnake (*Crotalus viridis nuntius*)	R	U,M
Mohave Rattlesnake (*Crotalus scutulatus*)	R	L

TURTLES

Spiny Softshell (*Apalone spinifera*; non-native)	R	L

KEY

Column 1 - **Abundance**
  A-Abundant, **C**-Common,
  E-Extirpated, **N**-Uncommon,
  P-Population re-established,
  R-Rare.
Column 2 - **Distribution**
  U-Upper Canyon, **M**-Middle,
  L-Lower, **T**-Throughout,
  LF-Lees Ferry, **DC**-Diamond Cr.

First Tiger Salamander found in the Colorado River, Mile -9L March 2015.

Seven of the 10 species of lizards occurring in the river corridor are commonly observed during the daylight hours (Table 5.2). Four additional lizard species, not included in Table 5.2, live at higher elevations in Grand Canyon. The common river corridor lizards are niche-specific and usually can be identified by referring to Plate 5F.

At least 17 species of snakes occur in the river corridor, but most are rarely encountered and many are known only from a few specimens (Table 5.2).[205] The most commonly encountered snakes in the eastern basin are the rather docile Grand Canyon (pink) Rattlesnake (*Crotalus oreganus abyssus*), its black-and-white-banded predator the California Kingsnake (*Lampropeltus getulus*), the Striped Whipsnake (*Masticophis taeniatus*), and the Gopher Snake (*Pituophis catenifer*). Hopi Rattlesnakes (*C. viridis nuntius*) are rare. Western Grand Canyon supports five rattlesnakes, of which Speckled Rattlesnake (*Crotalus mitchellii*) is most common. It closely resembles the Grand Canyon Rattlesnake, but its blotches wrap fully around the body. Other lower Canyon species include Western Diamondback (*Crotalus atrox*), Mohave (*C. scutulatus*), Black-tailed (*C. molossus*), and Great Basin (*C. oreganus lutosus)* Rattlesnakes. Banded Gila Monsters (*Heloderma suspectum cinctum*) only occur downstream from Mile 200, primarily on river left. The only turtle in the river corridor is the non-native, now-rare Spiny Soft-shelled Turtle (*Apalone spinifera*), which comes upriver from Lake

Table 5.3
Common or Distinctive Birds of the CRE

American Coot	C	I	T	Y
Western Grebe	N	I	T	Y
Double-crested Cormorant	N	B,I	M,L	Y
Great Blue Heron	C	B,I	T	Y
Snowy Egret	N	I	T	Y
Black-crowned Night Heron	N	I	M,L	F,S
Canada Goose	C	M	T	W
Blue-winged Teal	C	B,M,I	T	Y
Cinnamon Teal	C	M,I	T	Y
Green-winged Teal	C	M,I	T	Y
Common Goldeneye	C	M,I	U,M	W
Bufflehead	C	M,I	U,M	W
Mallard	C	B,M,I	U	Y
Gadwall	C	I	U	W
American Widgeon	C	I	U	Y
Turkey Vulture	C	I	T	SF,S
Cooper's Hawk	N	I	T	FS
Red-tailed Hawk	C	B	T	SF,S
Golden Eagle	N	B	T	Y
Bald Eagle	N	I	U,M	W
Osprey	N	M	U,M	FS,W
Prairie Falcon	R	B	T	SF,S

Table 5.3
Common or Distinctive Birds of the CRE in Lower Glen Canyon and Grand Canyon

Species	Abundance	Status	Distribution	Season
Peregrine Falcon	N	B	T	SF,S
American Kestrel	N	B	T	SF,S
Killdeer	N	M,I	T	SF
Spotted Sandpiper	C	B	T	SF,S
American Avocet	N	M	T	SF
Black-necked Stilt	N	M	T	SF
Common Snipe	N	M	T	SF
Red-necked Phalarope	N	M	T	SF
Wild Turkey	R	R	M,L	Y
Gamble's Quail	R	B	L	Y
Mourning Dove	A	B	T	SF,S
Greater Roadrunner	R	R,B?	T	Y
White-throated Swift	A	B	T	SF,S
Black-chinned Hummingbird	C	B	T	SF,S
Anna's Hummingbird	C	B	T	SF,S
Costa's Hummingbird	C	B	T	SF,S
Belted Kingfisher	N	M	T	SF,W
Red-naped Sapsucker	N	I	T	W
Northern Flicker	N	M	T	SF,W
Ladder-backed Woodpecker	N	B	U,M	SF,S
Ash-throated Flycatcher	A	R	T	SF,F
Black Phoebe	A	B	T	Y
Say's Phoebe	A	B	T	Y
Southwestern Willow Flycatcher	R	M	T	SF,S
Phainopepla	N	B	L	Y
Violet-green Swallow	A	B,I	T	SF,S
Cliff Swallow	N	I	U	SF,F
Northern Rough-winged Swallow	N	B	T	U,L
Scrub Jay	N	M,I	T	W
Common Raven	C	B	T	Y
Pinyon Jay	N	I	T	SF,W
Mountain Chickadee	C	M,I	U,M	SF,W
Common Bushtit	C	M,I	T	SF,W
American Dipper	N	B	U,M	Y
Canyon Wren	A	R,B	T	Y
Marsh Wren	N	M,I	T	SF,W
Rock Wren	A	R,B	T	Y
Blue-gray Gnatcatcher	C	B	T	SF,S
Ruby-crowned Kinglet	C	M,I	T	SF,W
Bell's Vireo	C	B	T	SF,S
Lucy's Warbler	A	B	T	SF,S
Yellow Warbler	C	B	T	SF,S
Yellow-rumped Warbler	A	M	T	SF,W
Common Yellowthroat	C	B	T	SF,S
Yellow-breasted Chat	C	B	T	SF,S
House Sparrow	N	B	M	Y
Red-winged Blackbird	N	M,I	T	SF,S
Hooded Oriole	N	B	T	SF,S
Northern Oriole	N	B	T	SF,S
Great-tailed Grackle	C	R,B	U,M	SF,S
Brown-headed Cowbird	C	B	T	SF,S
Northern Mockingbird	N	B	U,L	SF,S
Western Tanager	N	M,I	T	SF
Blue Grosbeak	N	B	T	SF,S
Lazuli Bunting	N	B	T	SF,S
House Finch	A	B,I	T	Y
Lesser Goldfinch	C	B	T	SF,S
Spotted Towhee	N	I	T	W
Black-throated Sparrow	A	B	T	SF,S
Dark-eyed Junco	A	M,I	T	SF,W
White-crowned Sparrow	A	M,I	T	SF,W
Lincoln's Sparrow	C	M,I	T	Y
Vesper Sparrow	C	M,I	T	SF,W
Song Sparrow	N	B	U,L	SF,S

KEY

Column 1 - **Abundance:** **A**-Abundant, **C**-Common, **N**-Uncommon, **R**-Rare.
Column 2 - **Status:** **B**-Breeding, **I**-Itinerant, **M**-Migrant, **R**-Resident year-round
Column 3 - **Distribution:** **U**-Upper, **M**-Middle, **L**-Lower, **T**-Throughout
Column 4 - **Season:** **SF**-Spring and Fall, **S**-Summer, **W**-Winter, **Y**-Year-round

Razorback Sucker

The endangered razorback sucker (*Xyrauchen texanus*) is a large, mainstream fish species that ranged widely through the Colorado River basin in pre-dam time.[206] Growing to more than 2 ft (0.6 m) in length, it may live more than 40 yr. Adults bear a pronounced dorsal keel. Like humpback chub, the sucker's dorsal keel was believed to stabilize navigation in swift, turbulent waters, but experimental studies fail to show such a benefit and suggest the elevated dorsal keel reduces the likelihood of predation by Colorado Pikeminnow (*Ptychocheilus lucius*).[227] Old, large individuals still exist in Lakes Mohave and Mead, but recent monitoring in lowermost Grand Canyon has revealed more Razorback Sucker below Mile 240. In 2014 the NPS released Razorback Suckers below Lava Falls to track adult movement, and discovered more larval suckers below Lava Falls and further downstream. Thus this once-rare fish is now more abundant than previously thought.

Mead as far as Mile 243. In pre-dam time, turtles (perhaps Painted Turtles - *Chrysemys picta*) also were reported at the mouth of the Paria River and in the lower San Juan River.[1]

Birds: The post-dam profusion of riverside vegetation greatly boosted the number and abundance of bird species in the Canyon (Table 5.3).[36,168, 261, 280] In addition, a few species such as Bald Eagles (*Haliaeetus leucocephalus*), Common Raven (*Corvus corax*), Bell's Vireo (*Vireo belli*), Hooded Orioles (*Icterus cucullatus*), and Great-tailed grackles (*Quiscalus mexicanus*) have expanded their spatial or temporal ranges into the Canyon. Thus far, nearly 250 species of birds have been observed along the river, but most are non-breeding migrants or transient species.

Surprising avian appearances in the river corridor in recent decades have included Harlequin Duck (*Histrionicus histrionicus*), Great Frigatebird (*Fregata minor*), Scissor-tailed Flycatcher (*Tyrannus forficatus*), and Painted Bunting (*Passerina ciris*). Prior to 1963. early residents of Lees Ferry and predam river runners reported few aquatic and semi-aquatic birds in Grand Canyon; however, unanticipated post-dam increases in water clarity, aquatic vegetation and invertebrates, and shoreline vegetation cover have provided habitat for 60 waterbird species, including waterfowl, waders, shorebirds, picivorous raptors, and Belted Kingfishers.[261, 280] The clear waters of Lake Powell and the Glen Canyon Reach also attract great numbers of migratory and stopover waterfowl from November through March. Bald Eagles were rarely reported from the river corridor prior to 1982, but thereafter became regular winter visitors in the upper Canyon.[34, 35] During summer, Mallards now breed in nearly every large eddy down to the LCR, and summer flotillas of ducklings are commonly seen.[280]

Mammals:[241, 289] At least 50 native mammal species have been detected along the river, of which at least two species have recently disappeared. Mammals that are known only from the Rims or from the Grand Wash Cliffs area have not been included in Table 5.4.

River corridor mammal species are well adapted to their preferred habitats, but most are nocturnal and therefore are rarely seen.

At least 17 bat species are known from the Canyon, although they are poorly documented.[270] Of the 16 rodent species present along the river corridor, Rock Squirrels, Beaver (*Castor canadensis*), Canyon and Cactus Mice (*Peromyscus crinitus, P. eremicus*), and packrats (*Neotoma* spp.) are the most abundant,[241,289] and Muskrats (*Ondatra zibethicus*) are increasing. Rodent populations, including Beaver likely have increased dramatically as a result of the post-dam expansion of riparian vegetation. As prey populations increased, small carnivores such as Coyotes (*Canis latrans*), Gray Foxes (*Urocyon cinereoargenteus*), and Ringtails (*Bassariscus astutus*) have become more prevalent. Ringtails (Arizona's state mammal) are surprisingly abundant along the river, but are so strictly nocturnal that they are rarely observed. Agile and bold, they live in rock piles and ledges, and small, paired, cat-like tracks are commonly seen around camp after their wild midnight escapades. Mountain lions (*Puma concolor*), Gray Wolves (*Canis lupus*), and Bobcats (*Lynx rufus*) were largely or entirely eliminated from the North Rim during a federal predator control program between 1906 and 1926.[237] Although not common along the river, the cats are present in low numbers, and lions occasionally swim across the river. Sonoran River Otter (*Lontra canadensis sonora*) were rare in pre-dam time, and are likely now extinct.[1,241] Badger (*Taxidea taxus*) occurred along the upper river and recently have been documented above Lees Ferry, but apparently have been extirpated from Grand Canyon National Park.[1] Mule deer (*Odocoileus hemionus*) are common in wide reaches, and Grand Canyon and adjacent eastern Lake Mead support the largest remaining natural population of Desert Bighorn Sheep (*Ovis canadensis nelsoni*). A Collared Peccary (*Peccari tajacu*) skull was found mid-way up Spring Canyon (Mile 204.5R) in 2001, and a reliable sighting of a White-nosed Coati was reported there in 2016.

Southwestern Willow Flycatcher

The endangered Southwestern Willow Flycatcher (*Empidonax trailii extimus*) is a small, greenish flycatcher with white wing bars and an upright roosting posture. Formerly rarely breeding in Marble Canyon, it has been extirpated since about 2000 due to habitat degradation and brood parasitism by cowbirds (*Molothrus* spp.).[34,257] The recent invasion of Tamarisk Leaf Beetle in northern Arizona threatens remaining birds with further loss of habitat in the river corridor.

National Park Service

Peregrine Falcon

With a Latin moniker of *Falco peregrinus*, the "wandering scythe," Peregrine Falcons are the fastest creature on Earth, reaching speeds of 230 mph (370 km/hr) during their spectacularly raptorial stoops on waterfowl and other prey. Grand Canyon now supports the largest breeding concentration of Peregrines in any land unit in the coterminous United States.[35a,285]

Table 5.4
Mammals of the Colorado River corridor in Lower Glen Canyon and Grand Canyon

BATS

Yuma Myotis (*Myotis yumanensis*)	C	T
California Myotis (*Myotis californicus*)	C	U,M
Silver-haired Bat (*Lasionycteris noctivagans*)	R	M,L
Western Pipistelle (*Pipistrellus hesperus*)	N	T
Big Brown Bat (*Eptesicus fuscus*)	N	M,L
Townsend's Big-eared Bat (*Corynorhinus townsendi*)	R	U,M
Pallid Bat (*Antrozous pallidus*)	C	T
Mexican Free-tailed Bat (*Tadarida brasiliensis*)	C	T
Spotted Bat (*Euderma maculata*)	N	T
Allen's Big-eared Bat (*Idionycteris phyllotis*)	R	U,M
Big Free-tailed Bat (*Myctinomops macrotis*)	C	T
Cave Myotis (*Myotis velifer*)	R	L
Fringed Myotis (*Myotis thysanodes*)	R	U,M
Greater Western Mastiff Bat (*Eumops periotis*)	N	M
Hoary Bat (*Lasionycteris cinereus*)	R	T
Mexican Long-tongued Bat (*Choeronycteris mexicana*)	R	U
Western Red Bat (*Lasiurus blossevillii*)	R	L

CARNIVORES

Coyote (*Canis latrans*)	N	T
Gray Fox (*Urocyon cinereoargenteus*)	C	T
Ringtail (*Bassariscus astutus*)	C	T
Raccoon (*Procyon lotor*)	R	M,L
White-nosed Coati (*Nasua narica*)	S	L
Western Spotted Skunk (*Spilogale gracilis*)	N	T
Hog-nosed Skunk (*Conepatus mesoleucus*)	S	L
Badger (*Taxidea taxus*)	E	U
River Otter (*Lontra canadensis sonora*)	E	T
Mountain Lion (*Puma concolor*)	R	T
Bobcat (*Lynx rufus*)	R	T
Black Bear (*Ursus americanus*)	S	M,L

LAGOMORPHS

Desert Cottontail (*Sylvilagus audubonii*)	C	LF,LM
Black-tailed Jackrabbit (*Lepus californicus*)	C	LF,LM

RODENTS

Rock Squirrel (*Ammospermophilus spilosoma*)	C	T
Harris's Antelope Squirrel (*Ammospermophilus harrisii*)	R	M,L
White-tailed Antelope Squirrel (*Ammospermophilus leucurus*)	N	U,M
Cliff Chipmunk (*Eutamias dorsalis*)	N	M,L
White-throated Woodrat (*Neotoma albigula*)	A	U,M
Desert Woodrat (*Neotoma lepida*)	A	T
Long-tailed Pocket Mouse (*Chaetodipus formosus*)	N	T
Rock Pocket Mouse (*Chaetodipus intermedius*)	C	T
Western Harvest Mouse (*Reithrodontomys megalotis*)	R	U
Canyon Mouse (*Peromyscus crinitus*)	A	T
Cactus Mouse (*Peromyscus eremicus*)	A	T
Deer Mouse (*Peromyscus maniculatus*)	R	T
Brush Mouse (*Peromyscus boylii*)	N	T
Pinyon Mouse (*Peromyscus truei*)	R	M,L
Muskrat (*Ondatra zibethicus*)	R	U,L
Beaver (*Castor canadensis*)	C	T

ARTIODACTYLA

Mule Deer (*Odocoileus hemionus*)	C	M,L
Desert Bighorn Sheep (*Ovis canadensis nelsoni*)	C	T
Collared Peccary (*Pecari tajacu*)	S	L

PERISSODACTYLA

Feral Burro (*Equus asinus*)	R,E	L

Plate 5A: **Flowering Shrubs**

California Redbud
(*Cercis occidentalis*)

Stan Shebs

Brittlebush
(*Encelia farinosa*)

Stan Shebs

Dogweed
(*Thymnophylla pentachaeta*)

Catclaw
(*Acacia greggii*)

Stan Shebs

Mesquite
(*Prosopsis glandulossa* var. *torreyana*)

Don A. W. Carlson

Desert Pepperweed
(*Lepidium fremontii*)

Stan Shebs

Spiny Goldenweed
(*Xanthisma spinulosum*)

Stan Shebs

Ocotillo
(*Fouquieria splendens*)

Rock Nettle
(*Eucnide rupestris*)

Stan Shebs

Tamarisk
(*Tamarix chinensis x ramosissima*)

Tim Carlson / Tamarisk Coalition

McDougall's Flaveria
(*Flaveria mcdougallii*)

Stan Shebs

Creosotebush
(*Larrea tridentata*)

Blackbrush
(*Coleogyne ramosissima*)

National Park Service

Arroweed
(*Pluchea sericea*)

Stan Shebs

Bear-grass
(*Nolina microcarpa*)

Sally and Andy Wasowski
Lady Bird Johnson Wildflower Center

Spearleaf Bricklebush
(*Brickellia atractyloides*)

Stan Shebs

Plate 5B: **Wildflowers**

Globe Mallow
(*Sphaeralcea ambigua*)
Stan Shebs

Watercress
(*Nasturtium officinale*)

Heronbill
(*Erodium cicutarium*)

Desert Plume
(*Stanleya pinnata*)
USDA

Cardinal Monkeyflower
(*Mimulus cardinalis*)

Golden Monkeyflower
(*Mimulus cardinalis*)

Golden Columbine
(*Aquilegia chrysantha*)
Stan Shebs

Heleborine Orchid
(*Epipactus gigantea*)
Stan Shebs

Sand Verbena
(*Abronia elliptica*)

Colorado Four o'clock
(*Mirabilis multiflora*)
Stan Shebs

Evening Primrose
(*Oenothera pallida*)
Al Schneider @ USDA-NRCS PLANTS

Hooker's Primrose
(*Oenothera elata hookeri*)
Stan Shebs

Trailing Four o'clock
(*Allionia incarnata*)
Stan Shebs

Palmer's Penstemon
(*Penstemon palmeri*)

Scorpionweed
(*Phacelia crenulata*)
Stan Shebs

Buckley's Centaury
(*Zeltnera calycosa*)

Cardinal Flower
(*Lobelia cardinalis*)

Sacred Datura
(*Datura wrightii*)

Plate 5C: **Cacti and Yuccas**

Fishhook Cactus
(*Mammillaria* sp.)

Hedgehog (Claret Cup) Cactus
(*Echinocereus triglochidiatus*)

Pancake-pear
(*Optunia chlorotica*)

Beavertail Cactus
(*Opuntia basilaris*)

Engleman's Prickly-pear
(*Opuntia phaecantha*)

Teddybear Cholla
(*Opuntia bigelovii*)

Cotton Top Cactus
(*Echinocactus polycephalus*)

Mojave Prickly-pear
(*Opuntia erinacea*)

Banana Yucca
(*Yucca baccata*)

Narrowleaf Yucca
(*Yucca baileyi*)

Barrel Cactus
(*Ferocactus acanthodes*)

Grizzly Bear Prickly-pear
(*Opuntia polyacantha var. erinacea*)

Plate 5D: **Showy Insects**

Monarch Butterfly
(*Danaus plexippus*)

Queen Butterfly
(*Danaus gilippus*)

Arizona Sister
(*Adelpha eulalia*)

Buckeye
(*Junonia coenia*)

Acastus Patch
(*Chlosyne acastus*)

Lined Sphinx Moth
(*Hyles lineata*)

Mourning Cloak
(*Nymphalis antiopa*)

Many-tailed Swallowtail
(*Papilio multicaudata*)

Old World Swallowtail
(*Papilio machaon*)

Painted Lady
(*Vanessa cardui*)

Tarantula Hawks
(*Pepsis, Hemipepsis* spp.)

Vulnerable Rubyspot Damselfly
(*Hetaerina vulnerata*)

Flame Skinner Dragonfly
(*Libellula saturata*)

Velvet Ants
(*Mutillidae*)

Aquatic Insects
(*Thermonectus marmoratus*) - left
(*Notonecta lobata*) - middle
(*Hydrochara lineata*) - right

Butterfly photos, courtesy of Tom Chekinis

Plate 5E: **Native Fishes**

US Fish and Wildlife Service

Bluehead Sucker
(*Catostomus discobolus*)

Flannelmouth Sucker
(*Catostomus latipinnis*)

BioWest

Razorback Sucker
(*Xyrauchen texanus*)
Endangered

George Andrejko

Humpback Chub
(*Gila cypha*)
Endangered

Brian Gratwicke

Bonytail Chub
(*Gila elegans*)
Extirpated, Endangered

US Fish and Wildlife Service

Roundtail Chub
(*Gila robusta*)
Extirpated

US Fish and Wildlife Service

Colorado Pikeminnow
(*Ptychocheilus lucius*)
Extirpated, Endangered

Speckled Dace
(*Rhinichthys osculus*)

Three of the eight native fish species in Grand Canyon have been extirpated since the construction of Glen Canyon Dam.

Plate 5F: Amphibians and Reptiles

Canyon Treefrog
(*Hyla arenicolor*)

Red-spotted Toad
(*Anaxyrus punctatus*)

Rocky Mountain Toad
(*Anaxyrus woodhousii*)

Side-blotched Lizard
(*Uta stansburiana*)

Chuckwalla
(*Sauromalus ater*)

Yellow-backed Spiny Lizard
(*Sceloporus magister*)

Banded Gila Monster
(*Heloderma suspectum cinctum*)

Tree Lizard
(*Urosaurus ornatus*)

Northern Tiger Whiptail
(*Aspidoscelis tigris*)

Banded Gecko
(*Coleonyx variegatus*)

Eastern Collared Lizard
(*Crotaphytus collaris*)

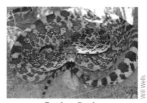

Gopher Snake
(*Pituophis catenifer*)

California Kingsnake
(*Lampropeltis getulus*)

Grand Canyon Rattlesnake
(*Crotalus oreganus abyssus*)

VI: THE RIVER AND THE DAM

Introduction: Managing the Wild

Grand Canyon is huge, harsh, and glorious: it is one of the world's most iconic and widely beloved landscapes. To Native Americans, each part and the whole of this place is a living entity. Reverence and protection of the Canyon in its natural state are paramount to many of us, including even those who have not seen it. Grand Canyon is designated a National Park and a United Nations World Heritage Site, with protection reaffirmed through the 1992 Grand Canyon Protection Act. Yet the Colorado River ecosystem (CRE) is highly modified by Glen Canyon Dam and other upstream dams. The river is the primary supply of water and an important source of energy for the entire Southwest. Enormous societal efforts and a bewildering array of advisors have endeavored to recommend ways to balance the many competing demands on the river. Below, we explore the pre-dam river, its impoundment by Glen Canyon Dam, post-dam responses, and present-day efforts to adaptively manage and conserve this extraordinary socio-ecosystem.

Glen Canyon Dam: A 50-Year Retrospective

Fifteen-and-a-half narrow, winding miles upstream from Lees Ferry, Glen Canyon Dam stands in flat, brilliant sunlight and deep shadows. Upstream, stretching for 180 miles (290 km) lie the deep, still waters of Lake Powell, which now fill Glen Canyon. The dam's alabaster, eye-stretching upward sweep makes the Navajo Sandstone look somehow ordinary, plain and red. From beneath the dam's concrete feet the river swirls up in a cool, sleepy, blue-green blush, roils around and runs into an eddy or two, and then wanders off downstream. Glen Canyon Dam is a modern technological wonder, a symbol of our culture, and is well worth seeing if you have the time.

The Power Kachina: color infrared aerial photograph of Glen Canyon dam, 1990.

Western Water Law and the Colorado River

Water law in the western United States is founded on the principle of appropriative rights: water is regarded as a commodity to be bought and sold, and can be wholly removed from its natural course for "beneficial use" by the senior owner of the water rights. The massive body of legal literature about the use of Colorado River water constitutes "the Law of the River," and is founded on the 1922 Colorado River Compact (Table 6.1),[56] which apportioned flow between the headwater Upper Basin (Colorado, Wyoming, Utah, and New Mexico) and the water-hungry Lower Basin (California, Arizona, and Nevada). The Compact designated Lee Ferry (one mile below the mouth of the Paria River, not to be confused with Lees Ferry) as the boundary between the Upper and Lower Basins. The 1956 Colorado River Storage Project Act (CRSP) authorized construction of seven major Upper Basin dams and reservoirs, and other water works projects.

Glen Canyon Dam Construction History and Design[56]

Glen Canyon Dam is the second largest dam in the US (Hoover is slightly bigger), and is by far the largest of the seven major CRSP dams. Preparation on the dam site began in 1956, and by early June 1960 the river was diverted by a coffer dam through tunnels drilled into the walls around the base of the site. Concrete was poured almost continuously by 2,500 workers for three and a quarter years. By 4 September 1963 when the dam was completed, nearly 5.4 million yd^3 (4.1 million m^3) of concrete had been sculpted into the massive structure that today rises 710 ft (217 m) above bedrock, and 583 feet (178 m) above the riverbed. A concrete arch dam, it curves *into* the lake, but it is 300 ft (91 m) thick at the base and could hold back the lake like a gravity dam even if it were not also set deeply into the canyon walls. To meet its flood control obligations, the dam was designed with a 138,000 cfs (3,908 m^3/s) spillway tunnel on either side and four hollow jet tubes at the base with a combined release capacity of 15,000 cfs (425 m^3/s). Thus the total bypass release capacity of the dam and the emergency release capacity is nearly 325,000 cfs (9,204 m^3/s), considerably higher than the 100-yr flood of 210,000 cfs (5,947 m^3/s). Power generation from Glen Canyon Dam began in September 1964, and on 22 September 1966 the dam and powerplant were dedicated by First Lady Claudia "Lady Bird" Johnson,

Table 6.1: Timeline of federal legislation and actions related to Glen Canyon Dam history and management.

1902 National Reclamation Act – established the Bureau of Reclamation to oversee the construction and maintenance of irrigation projects, leading to the impoundment of nearly every large river in the western US.

1906 Antiquities Act – Preservation of American antiquities

1916 National Park Service Organic Act – established the National Park Service

1919 Grand Canyon National Park created

1922 Colorado River Compact – defined how river flows were divided among Upper and Lower Colorado River basins

1928 Boulder Canyon Project Act – authorized Boulder (Hoover) Dam, allocation of Lower Basin waters; Secretary of the Interior as Water Master

1935 Boulder/Hoover Dam completed

1944 Water Treaty with Mexico – Mexico is to receive 1.5 maf, except during extreme droughts

1948 Upper Colorado River Basin Compact – apportioned flow among Upper Basin states

1956 Colorado River Storage Project Act – Authorized upper basin water storage projects, including 3 in Curecanti segment (upper Colorado River), two in upper Green River, Navajo Dam on San Juan River, and Glen Canyon Dam.

1963 Glen Canyon Dam completed on 13 September

1964 Arizona v. California US Supreme Court Decision – Lower Basin states can use tributary flows before those flows reach the Colorado River; Wilderness Act passed; Glen Canyon Dam produces power on 4 September

1968 Colorado River Basin Project Act – authorized Central AZ Project; Sec. of Interior to develop long-term operating criteria for reservoir and storage projects; Marble Canyon Dam plans permanently shelved, Bridge Canyon Dam plans abandoned

1969-70 National Environmental Policy Act; Clean Air Act (1970)

1972 Clean Water Act

1973 Endangered Species Act; Minute 242, US-Mexico International Boundary and Water Commission stipulated that water leaving Morelos Dam have an annual average salinity of ≤115 + 30 ppm

1974 Colorado River Basin Salinity Control Act – authorized construction of salinity control and desalinization project near Yuma

1992 Grand Canyon Protection Act – reaffirms the protection of Grand Canyon: "The Secretary shall operate Glen Canyon Dam in accordance with the additional criteria and operating plans…in such a manner as to protect, mitigate adverse impacts to, and improve the values for which Grand Canyon National Park and Glen Canyon National Recreation Area were established, including, but not limited to natural and cultural resources and visitor use."

1995-96 Glen Canyon Dam EIS completed and ROD ratified, reducing daily flow variability to conserve natural resources (sandbars, endangered humpback chub), Federal Advisory Committee Adaptive Management Workgroup (AMWG) to advise the Secretary of Interior on dam operations; high flow experiment (HFE) conducted

2007 Colorado River Interim Guidelines for…Shortages; and Coordinated Operations…authorized Reclamation to develop shortage strategies for coordinated management of Lakes Powell and Mead

2010 Minute 318, US-Mexico International Boundary and Water Commission allowed Mexico to store allocated water in Lake Mead during earthquake repairs

2011 AMWG's Desired Future Conditions for CRE to Secretary, which are accepted

2012 HFE criteria approved and 4th HFE conducted

2016 Long Term Experimental Management Plan EIS and ROD approved

who insisted that the dam be beautified (hence the green lawn at the dam's base).

Glen Canyon National Recreation Area was established in 1972, including Lake Powell, lower Cataract Canyon, and the surrounding desert lands in Arizona and Utah—a total land area slightly larger than Grand Canyon National Park. Lake Powell reservoir, "the jewel of the Colorado," has a surface area of 266 mi^2 (689 km^2) and a 1,960 mi (3,154 km)-long shoreline. At full pool, Lake Powell reservoir extends 186 mi (299 km) upstream, with a depth of 560 ft (171 m) at the dam.

The Bureau of Reclamation maintains Glen Canyon Dam and normal annual releases are 8.23 million ac-ft (maf; 10.15 km^3), of which 7.5 maf (9.25 km^3) is released to meet 1922 Compact obligations, and 0.73 maf (0.9 km^3) is released for the 1944 Water Treaty with Mexico. Since 1972 the Department of Energy's Western Area Power Administration has marketed the dam's hydroelectric power, selling to municipalities, rural electric cooperatives, Native American Tribes, and governmental agencies in Wyoming, Utah, Colorado, New Mexico, Arizona, Nevada, and Nebraska. Completed at a cost of $245 million, construction funds were provided through a 50-yr low-interest loan to be repaid by power revenues. The dam has a generation capacity of 1,320 KW, and produces five billion KW-hr annually for 130 utility and irrigation companies and their more than 5 million customers. Although Glen Canyon Dam provides only about 5% of the western grid's power supply, it is a made-to-order "peaking power" facility that can provide quick increases or decreases in electricity production through adjustment of the water flow through the turbines. The timing of demand for electricity varies seasonally, with mid-day demand in summer for air conditioning, and increased early morning and evening demand for heating in winter. The dam releases more water at midday than at night, creating an ecologically novel "daily river tide" (Fig. 6.1).

Bureau of Reclamation

First Lady, Mrs. Lyndon B. Johnson, dedicates Glen Canyon Dam – 1966.

Reflections on Colorado River Ecosystem: Alteration and Management

The post-dam river is much different from pre-dam times. A group of pre-dam river runners were invited on a river trip by the USGS in 1994 to observe post-dam changes.[329] They reported colder river water temperature, nearly clear flows, much sand bar erosion, tamarisk invasion, reduction in the amount of driftwood, expansion of riverside marshes, increased non-native fish as compare to native species, and increased abundance of waterbirds. These changes generally reflect the range of ecological and biological transitions noted in a host of scientific studies, and reconfirm the magnitude of difference before and after completion of Glen Canyon Dam.

The dam stabilized the river ecosystem, increasing terrestrial biodiversity, but decoupling it from climate. The dam also may be reducing long-term nutrient flux through the CRE. However, the dam affects webs of life in the water and on the land differently. Flow regulation largely swamped the influences of geomorphology, reducing differences in the composition of aquatic biota among aquatic microhabitats. In contrast, flow regulation enhanced variation in habitat and biological diversity in the riparian domain.[279] Differential aquatic vs. terrestrial responses of the river ecosystem to flow regulation greatly complicate stewardship of focal species and habitats.[173, 245, 283]

Figure 6.1[106]
The shape of the kinematic (pressure) wave of highly fluctuating daily flows from Glen Canyon Dam changes over distance downstream. In contrast, the rate of water movement is much slower and depends on the magnitude of release: water movement is indicated by the dots showing dye movement. Redrawn from Graf (1995).

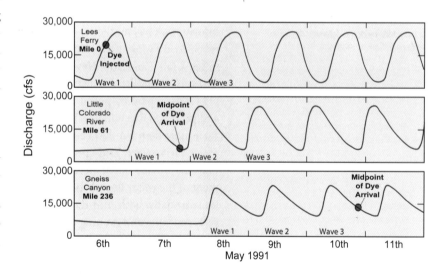

How It Was and How It Is: The Pre-dam and Post-dam Colorado Rivers

River Flows at Lees Ferry

Pre-dam Flows: The pre-dam Colorado River was seasonally warm and sediment-laden with a large spring snowmelt flood, erratic summertime flows, and low flows from November-March.[129, 295] Tree ring-based reconstruction of river flows for Lees Ferry from 762 CE to the present (Fig. 6.2) demonstrates enormous variability in annual flow and prolonged droughts, nine of which lasted 15–20yr.[111, 197] The historic record of predam Colorado River flows at Lees Ferry includes anecdotal and USGS streamflow data since 1921.[219, 295] Floods and droughts in the Colorado River Basin are related to El Nino warming of the southern Pacific Ocean surface and snowpack in the Rocky Mountains. [314, 326, 330]

Instantaneous flows at Lees Ferry varied tremendously within the year (Figs. 6.3, 6.4).[295] Winter low flows at Lees Ferry in historic times varied from 1,000-5,000 cfs (28-140 m³/s), increasing to an annual June peak flow typically in excess of 50,000 cfs (1,415 m³/s). Dry years like 1934 had low maximum peak flows of only 25,507 cfs (722 m³/s) and brought in only 4.4 million acre-feet (maf; 5.43 km³). The maximum historic flood recorded was 210,000 cfs (5,947 m³/s) in 1884, the springtime after the volcano Krakatoa erupted in Indonesia, and a flow of 170,000 cfs (4,814 m³/s) occurred in 1921. High inflow years may deliver in excess of 22 maf (27.1 km³). Although pre-dam mainstream flows varied little within days,[295] the Colorado River varied by nearly two orders of magnitude over 2–4 week intervals (Fig. 6.2, 6.3).

Cumulative annual inflow at Lees Ferry, just upstream from the Upper-Lower Basin boundary, is critical information for basin water management, but the 1922 Colorado River Compact famously over-allocated the flow of the river. Early estimates of basin discharge of 15 maf/yr (18.5 km³/yr) were considerably higher than the longer-term average.[129] Thus, the 1922 Compact places the entire Colorado River basin in a permanent water deficit, a challenge famously foreseen by John Wesley Powell. "… there is not sufficient water to irrigate all the lands which could be irrigated...I tell you, gentlemen, you are piling up a heritage of conflict" (address by Powell to the Los Angeles International Irrigation Conference, 1893).

Post-dam Flows: After 1965, the flow regime shifted from highly variable seasonal flows to highly variable daily flows, with little seasonal variation. (Fig. 6.1, 6.4) Post-dam daily flow commonly ranged from less than 3,000 cfs at night to 25,000–30,000 cfs during mid-day on weekdays, with low flows on weekends due to reduced hydroelectricity demand. Higher flows occurred in mid-winter for heating and in mid-summer for air-conditioning, with lower flows in springtime (when the river naturally would have been high) and late fall. Consequently, the dam decoupled and buffered the river from climate.

Post-dam high flows occurred either as "acts of God" or as management actions. In 1980, when the reservoir first filled, high flows were run to test spillways. However, 1983 caught river managers off guard. Late winter, early springtime storms filled to overflowing an already full Lake Powell. River flows increased from the top of pow-erplant capacity (33,000 cfs) to spillway releases. In late June, dam releases peaked at approximately 92,600 cfs (2,622 m³/s). These flows, equivalent to a pre-dam 3-yr flood, scoured sandbars and riparian vegetation, threatened the integrity of the dam, and resulted in the capsizing of four motor rigs in one day in Crystal Rapid. Above-powerplant-capacity flows were repeated each year from 1983 through 1986. After the high flows subsided, Reclamation repaired the spillways and excavated a vertical shaft from the cavitation point to vent pressure during spillway releases. Since that time, high flows have been avoided, except recently for high flow experiments.[198, 221, 328]

Water travels relatively slowly through the river corridor: parcels of water released from the dam during low flows of 5,000 cfs (142 m³/s) travel only 0.7 mi/hr (1.1 km/hr), whereas at a flow rate of 30,000 cfs (850 m³/s), the water parcel moves at about 3.0 mph (4.8 km/hr). Water parcels tend to remain intact in this geologically con-strained river, thus it can take a full day under low flows for water to travel from the dam to Lees Ferry, and 10 days or more for the water to move all the way through.[106]

In contrast, a kinematic (pressure) wave travels rapidly through the river corridor to Diamond Creek. A kinematic wave is similar to a ripple spreading out around a

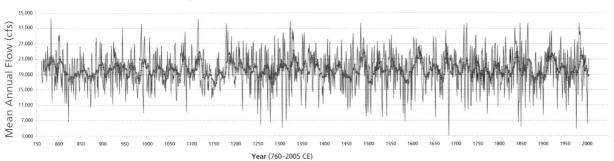

Figure 6.2
Mean annual flow (cfs) of the Colorado River at Lees Ferry, 750-2005 CE. Inner line is the rolling decadal average 10-yr flow

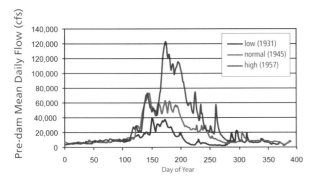

Figure 6.3
Average pre-dam daily flows (cfs) of the Colorado River at Lees Ferry during low (1931), normal (1945), and high (1957) inflow years.

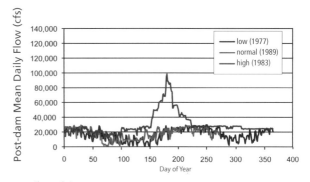

Figure 6.4
Average post-dam daily flows (cfs) of the Colorado River at Lees Ferry during low (1977), normal (1989), and high (1983) inflow years.

stone thrown into a slow-moving stream: the water surface remains slowly moving while the ripple quickly moves across it. Prior to 1991, the daily kinematic tide was up to 15 ft (5 m) in height in narrow reaches like the Upper Granite Gorge, but since 1991 the wave height has been reduced to about 4 ft/day (1.2 m/day). The timing of the daily rise and fall depends on one's location downstream. The tide wave moving at about 3-4 mph (5-6.5 km/hr), or 110 mi/day (175 km/day), normally begins to rise at Lees Ferry at about 9:00 a.m., takes a full day to reach Phantom Ranch, and takes about two days to reach Diamond Creek. The wave shape changes as it moves downstream (Fig. 6.1).[106] While regularly oscillating at the dam, the leading edge of the wave steepens to near vertical by the LCR, with wave height related to channel width. Thus the daily peaks rise increasingly quickly downstream. Ramping is the rate at which water releases change, and higher downramping rates increase seepage erosion.[38] However, this downstream-steepening wave front constrains effective regulation of ramping rates unless multiple-day flow management regimes are considered.

Sediment Transport

Pre-dam Sedimentology: Water has been the sculptor and primary agent of erosion in the Southwest, and the Colorado River has been the vehicle transporting eroded sediments off of the Plateau. The River has transported at least 74,420 mi³ (310,000 km³) of the Earth's crust over the past 10 m.y.[70]

The pre-dam Colorado River transported an annual average of 60 million metric tons (mt) of fine sediment transport/yr, mostly as silt and sand.[9] This is the equivalent of a 5-ton dump truck filled with mud and sand passing Phantom Ranch every 2.6 sec for a year! Under nearly natural flow conditions in Cataract Canyon upstream from Lake Powell, the Colorado River deposits enormous sandbars, usually eroding most of them away within a couple of months; however, high flows deposit sand at upper stage elevations, extending its residence time. Sand also blew upslope and protected archeological sites. Thus, fluvial erosion was dynamic in the unregulated Colorado River, cyclically depositing and eroding sandbars at specific sites related to the mouths of tributary canyons.

Post-dam Sedimentology: Virtually no suspended sediment passes through Glen Canyon Dam, all of it having settled out at the mouths of Lake Powell tributaries[296] Those sediment deposits shift, fail, and gradually move downslope towards the dam, but are far from the foot of the dam. Gramms et al.[108] reported that the bed of the Colorado River in the Glen Canyon Reach dropped by an average of 8.5 ft (2.6 m) after construction of Glen Canyon Dam. The bed began eroding and lowering in 1959 when the cofferdam was constructed, but most of the incision took place in 1965 when the Bureau of Reclamation ran a series of 14 pulsed high flows of up to 65,000 cfs (1,841 m³/s) to flush sand from around the base of the dam.

The three turbidity segments of the river have very different sediment transport regimes, and therefore different responses to post-dam sediment supply limitation.[281, 296] The clearwater segment from the Dam to the Paria River mouth is "sediment starved," and recovery of its sandbars has largely been written off. In contrast, the usually turbid segment downstream from the Little Colorado River still receives 10 million mt/yr of sand. The variably turbid segment between the Paria and Little Colorado River confluences is the main target for sandbar management. The Paria River delivers about 1.5 million mt/yr of fine sand,[107, 295a] a sediment load that moves out of that segment relatively quickly.[337]

Post-dam sandbar erosion has been widely recognized as a long-term consequence of flow regulation,[136, 337] and widely fluctuating hourly flows from 1965-1991 resulted in loss of more than 20% of sandbars in some reaches.[108, 109, 246] In addition to fluctuating flows, natural and boat-generated wave action and seepage erosion contribute to beach loss.[14, 38] Vegetation overgrowth also has become a leading cause of campsite loss.[159a] Sandbar loss due to dam operations has become a major focus for the USGS monitoring of sediment transport and mass balance, and sand storage is the primary purpose of high flow experiments.[198] Eolian (wind)-related sandbar deflation and the lack of sand available for eolian transport and covering archeological sites are related stewardship concerns.[73, 88]

The USGS formula for conservation of incoming Paria River sediment and mainstream sandbar maintenance involves keeping the river as low a discharge as possible to reduce sediment export. When sand is delivered during late summer monsoon floods, conducting a brief high flow experiment can be used to deposit sand at higher elevations in the channel, where it will be retained longer.[337] The downsides of this strategy are that it calls for sand-conserving low flows in summer (when dam profits are highest), accurate gauging of incoming sediment supplies (improved USGS gauging of the Paria River has helped), a rapid dam-response capability, and HFEs during late autumn (i.e., November) when they never occurred naturally. While HFEs allow for co-management of sediment mass balance with water storage, they are minor floods in comparison with natural, pre-dam floods. Thus, this strategy has shrunk the river ecosystem into a smaller spatial scope. The Secretary of the Interior approved HFE triggering criteria for 2012–2020, and we can expect more frequent, late autumn HFEs over the next decade to conserve camping beaches, archeological sites, and shoreline habitats in Grand Canyon.[309]

Water Temperature

Pre-dam Water Temperature: Colorado River water temperatures naturally varied greatly on a seasonal basis. The river froze occasionally in winter, and early settlers sometimes crossed their wagons over on the ice at Lees Ferry.[325] July water temperatures at Lees Ferry regularly reached 85 ° F (29° C), and may have exceeded 90° F (32° C) at Separation Rapid. Warm, turbid (silty) water reduces dissolved oxygen concentration and promotes microbial proliferation, and limits aquatic plant, insect, and fish production in the river.

Post-dam Water Temperature: As Lake Powell filled, the water temperature at Lees Ferry gradually cooled, reaching its present-day 47-50 °F (8-10 °C) condition by 1972. Since that time it has varied relatively little due to the water being released from the permanently cold hypolimnion (deep-water layer).[315] Water temperature increases slightly at the dam in autumn, during summer in years when the reservoir is low, and over distance downstream during the summer, depending on flow rate. Often by the time one reaches Diamond Creek in summer, the water temperature is tolerably above 60°F (16°C);[338] however, the river would need to flow unimpeded more than 600 miles (1,000 km) from Glen Canyon Dam to regain most of its annual temperature variability.[281] Mainstream temperature chills somewhat in the winter, but the river is warmer in winter than it was in pre-dam time.

Much has been made of the potential to warm the river to better support remaining native fish, which are all warm-water species. Temperature control devices (TCDs) have been used to support native fish populations in other rivers. However, growing concerns over differential benefits to non-native, warm-water fish, fish parasites, crayfish, and other invertebrate species have recently trumped calls for a TCD.

Rapids

Pre-dam Rapids: Only at a few sites, such as Waltenberg (Mile 113), 113.5 Mile, Bedrock (131), Helicopter Eddy (Mile 135.5) and 232 Mile Rapids does bedrock on the floor of the river directly withstand the river's erosional forces and form rapids. Most rapids are formed by debris flows—rare, large, tributary floods that transport huge boulders into the river. These slope-failure slurry-flows are generated when persistent rains saturate steep piles of eroded loose material called colluvium, particularly in the Hermit and Supai Formations. Debris flows that transport multi-ton boulders down channels can reach the mainstream, creating natural dams.[112, 327] As a general rule, larger tributaries typically have too low a gradient to transport debris flows: the Paria and Little Colorado Rivers, and Kanab and Havasu Creeks have produced only minor rapids. Normally, only a few large high-gradient tributaries send debris flows to the river in any individual year. For example, large debris flows reached the river at Red (Hance), National, Parashant, and Separation Canyons in 2012. However, exceptionally intense, longer-duration storms can spawn debris flows across large areas. One such storm was a rain-on-snow event over more than a week in early December 1966. Massive debris flows occurred in Nankoweap Creek and tributaries in the middle of the Upper Granite Gorge. The largest flood in a thousand years roared down Crystal Creek, washing immense boulders across the river, damming it, and turning a relatively minor rapid into an awesome cataract.[56a]

Post-dam Rapids: Prior to the dam, smaller tributary flood debris was regularly swept away in the mainstream's springtime floods. But now, with the river regulated, rapids tend to gain additional boulders, making their navigation more challenging. Once the relationship between tributary flooding and post-dam sediment transport was recognized, it was presumed that most new rapids would form due to debris flow activity. However, slope failure (wall collapse) events also spawn large, new rapids or worsen existing rapids, including Redneck (Mile 18, 1979), MNA (Mile 27, January 1975), the new President Harding (Mile 44, ~2000), and 209 Mile Rapid (1979).

The navigational severity of rapids changes individually in relation to flow, and there is no one flow regime safest for river running.[211] However, the biggest rapids generally become more challenging at higher flows. One rapid, Pearce Ferry, formed through a unique mechanism. Lake Mead was full in the late 1990s, and reservoir waters flooded the old Colorado River channel and low-lying parts of the surrounding landscape, depositing thick layers of silt and creating a new, level surface. Subsequent drought through the 2000s lead to historically low lake elevations and the entering river channelized its course, cutting down through silt deposits and over a bedrock exposure that lies outside of the former channel. By 2011, this bedrock constriction became a nearly unrunnable rapid. A Secretarial decision to balance reservoir elevations in 2011 partially refilled Lake Mead, and by late 2012 the rapid was submerged. However, lower reservoir stages in the past few years have made Pearce Ferry Rapid re-emerge, so don't miss the take-out!

The Aquatic Domain

Pre-dam Aquatic Domain: Little is known about pre-dam aquatic life in the Colorado River.[281] Woodbury's 1959[336] report on Glen Canyon aquatic insects mixed collections of specimens from the mainstream with those in the species-rich, springfed tributaries, leading to misinterpretation of predam invertebrate biodiversity. Invertebrate sampling upstream from Cataract Canyon shows that low-gradient riffles there support some dragonflies, hellgrammites, aquatic beetles, and aquatic flies, species that no longer occur in the mainstream in Grand Canyon.[125] Also, aquatic insects cling to driftwood and shoreline wood during floods,[124] but floating trees and other coarse woody debris have been largely eliminated in the post-dam CRE. Sand-dominated river floor habitats and high velocity cobble substrata in Cataract Canyon

are not particularly productive or rich in aquatic invertebrates, suggesting that the pre-dam Grand Canyon was similarly depauperate and relatively low in productivity. In contrast, cooler water tributaries, like Tapeats Creek and others on the north side of Grand Canyon, are rich in aquatic invertebrates.[218a] Therefore, predaceous fish like chubs and pikeminnows should have been detected primarily around tributary mouths, where pre-dam food resources existed in greater abundance. This pattern is generally supported by the historic fisheries evidence in Grand Canyon.

Post-dam Aquatic Domain: Water clarity increased in the Glen Canyon reach by 1972. For the first time in recent geological history, sunlight regularly reached the floor of the Colorado River. The clear, constantly cold but not freezing water in the Glen Canyon reach now supports a few, highly productive aquatic invertebrate taxa, including midges, buffalo gnats, and introduced scud and New Zealand mudsnails. Downstream, due to increasing turbidity and more variable water temperatures, the aquatic food web begins to resemble the natural, low productivity condition that likely characterized the pre-dam river.[25, 125, 135, 281, 287] The post-dam Colorado River has extremely low invertebrate biodiversity overall, with few caddisflies or other insects typical of clear, cold water. The post-dam river has lost three of its eight native fish species, with the last Colorado Pikeminnow reported from Havasu Creek in 1975 and Razorback Sucker recently reported in the lower canyon.[206] Populations of Flannelmouth and Bluehead Suckers, Speckled Dace, and endangerd Humpback Chub are healthy and increasing. Translocation of Humpback Chub by the NPS into Shinomu Creek failed due to flooding, but similar efforts have been partially successful in Havasu Creek.

The Riparian Domain

Pre-dam Riparian Zone: Pre-dam biological information, in contrast to physical data, is restricted to a few reports: the floristic studies of Clover and Jotter;[50] analyses of rematched historic photography;[267, 279, 297, 325, 331] reanalysis of pre-dam vegetation;[232, 279] and interviews, anecdotes, and analyses of early river runners and their diaries.[280, 329] Angus Woodbury lead four river ecology expeditions through Glen

Canyon in the late 1950s and documented the distribution of riparian vegetation and selected biota.[336]

Those studies show that the pre-dam river corridor was scoured by large, annual floods, and that little perennial vegetation existed along the lower riparian zone shoreline. Historic photographs show wide reaches of the river having middle and upper zones of riparian vegetation, and a few rare deciduous trees, like Goodding's tree willow (*Salix gooddingii*) present along the river.[47, 336] Perennial riparian vegetation was restricted upslope to terraces that were scoured more than every six years, and dominated by honey mesquite, catclaw, Apache-plume, and xeroriparian species. Radiocarbon dating of pre-dam upper riparian mesquite has revealed living plants more than 750 yr in age, and relatively small catclaw older than 400 yrs—making the mesquite zone an old-growth woodland. Non-native *Bromus* grasses came to dominance in the latter half of the 20th century. The desert vegetation today is similar to that depicted in photographs from a century or more ago, but has responded to occasional heavy freezes and prolonged drought.[325] Plants like Mormon tea (*Ephedra* spp.) may live for centuries, and often show little change in stature over 100 yr.[26] Early river runners and their diaries revealed a pre-dam river that supported a limited fishery, few beaver and otters, with some shorebirds and waterfowl.[280, 329] For example, Stanton[265] reported observing a flood-drowned beaver, while trappers Flavell and Montéz[95b] reported no beaver in 1896.

Together with little perennial riparian vegetation, poor fishing and few waterfowl or riparian wildlife, a portrait emerges of a wild but unproductive natural river. This picture is generally supported by matching pre-dam to post-dam historic photographs,[267, 297, 325] hunting and fishing reports, and observations in early river runner's diaries,[280, 336] and interviews with elders.[329]

Post-dam Riparian Zone: Biodiversity is predicted to increase when naturally highly disturbed ecosystems are ecologically stabilized, and such has been the case for the post-dam CRE.[274, 280] The post-dam riparian zone was transformed from a nearly barren shoreline to one now profusely vegetated and supporting many plant, invertebrate and vertebrate species.[149, 297] The upper riparian terrace zone, above the 10-yr flood stage, has changed least, although it is slowly being colonized by catclaw. The middle riparian zone, flooded on a 3–10-yr basis is being colonized by desert brittlebush and cacti, as well as lower riparian shrubs, like seepwillows (*Baccharis* spp.). The lower riparian zone was extensively colonized by tamarisk as early as 1970, which covered about 40% of the shorelines until 2011.[210]

The cover of fluvial marsh vegetation in the hydro-riparian zone underwent a dramatic expansion from 1965–1982, was nearly entirely scoured in 1983–1986, and then vigorously re-colonized from 1987–1995.[278-279] Since that time, infilling of backwaters, homogenization of nearshore sandy soils, and steepening shorelines has reduced habitat suitability for many marsh species. Recent flows have greatly favored the expansion of Common Reed and non-native Ripgut Brome (*Bromus rigidus*).

The riparian zone is still actively changing in post-dam time. The eruption of introduced Tamarisk Leaf Beetle (*Diorhabda carinulata*) is quickly decimating tamarisk stands, with unknown longer-term consequences.[277a] Beaver have reduced populations of native coyote willow (*Salix exigua*) and Goodding's tree willow. Many of the riparian plant species that depend on fine-grained wet substrate to germinate have declined as sand grain size has increased through winnowing by post-dam, clearwater floods, while plants that propagate through running roots, like Arrowweed (*Pluchea sericea*) and Common Reed are proliferating in the post-1991 riparian zone.[269, 278]

Wildlife also has responded dynamically. Double-crested Cormorants (*Phalacrocorax auritus*), Great Blue Herons (*Ardea herodias*), Mallards (*Anas platyrhynchos*), Common Mergansers (*Mergus merganser*), and Blue-winged Teal (*Anas discors*) breed in the river corridor.[280] Peregrine Falcons (*Falco peregrinus*) scream down onto their waterbird prey. Bald Eagles and 60 other waterbird species can be abundant in winter months in the upper reaches. Numerous small carnivores feed on abundant riparian rodents and insects, and Desert Mule Deer and Desert Bighorn Sheep are commonly seen along the river. All of these species have taken advantage of post-dam increases in riparian vegetation cover, ecosystem stability and productivity.[46, 241, 270, 289]

Adaptive Management of Glen Canyon Dam and the Colorado River

Glen Canyon Dam has had mixed impacts on the river ecosystem. Positive societal effects of the dam, such as power generation, improved recreation, and expanded wildlife habitat are countered by sandbar erosion, loss of native fish, lack of native riparian tree germination, and reduced wilderness quality.[283] Lees Ferry has become an important historic site and a blue-ribbon trophy trout fishery, and many thousands of anglers visit it each year to try their luck. The pre-dam river was a sea of churning mud, memorable but uninviting in flood, and a trickle during dry times. Now the cold, constrained, and often clear river is enjoyed by more than 70,000 visitors annually.[211]

The Department of the Interior's solution to stewardship of the river ecosystem, with its many conflicting environmental and economic values, is adaptive management of dam operations: applying information in a carefully considered, holistic ecosystem approach, using management actions as scientific experiments, learning by doing, and adjusting actions to new findings.[171, 321] The Glen Canyon Dam Adaptive Management Work Group (AMWG) was convened as a Federal Advisory Committee in 1997 to provide recommendations to the Secretary of the Interior on how best to balance environmental and economic values in the management of the dam (Fig. 6.5).[274, 308] The AMWG consists of a body of 27 stakeholder groups and federal agencies, including: Reclamation (the lead agency), NPS, US Fish & Wildlife Service, Bureau of Indian Affairs, five Native American Tribes, the Basin states, trout fishers, river runners (Grand Canyon River Guides), Grand Canyon Wildlands Council and National Parks Conservation Association. Members of the public are welcome to attend AMP meetings, which usually take place in Phoenix several times/yr (www.usbr.gov).

The 1996 Record of Decision (ROD) attempted to balance the environmental impacts of Glen Canyon Dam operations on the Colorado River Ecosystem (CRE) with hydroelectric power generation.[202, 308] The modified low, fluctuating flows (MLFF) alternative contained the following constraints: flows not less than 8,000 cfs (226 m³/s) between 7:00 a.m. and 7:00 p.m. (but down to 5,000 cfs—142 m³/s—for six hours at night); maximum releases of 20,000 cfs (566 m³/s); seasonally adjusted ranges of daily flow fluctuation, from 5,000–8,000 cfs/24 hr; and up-ramping not to exceed 2,500 cfs (70.5 m³/s)/hr and down-ramping of less than 1,500 cfs (42.3 m³/s)/hr to minimize seepage erosion (under rapidly down-ramping flows, water stored in sandbars tends to flow out quickly, creating cutbanks and widespread calving erosion).[38] MLFF allows for high flow experiments (HFEs) to store sand along the channel margins.

A decadal review of the MLFF flow regime produced mixed results.[173] The MLFF regime has not allowed a sufficient reserve of sand to accumulate in the channel for building sandbars using high flows,[337] therefore more frequent rapid-response HFEs are needed. The Canyon's Humpback Chub population appears to be recovering, and much insight into future research needs has been gained.

The 2016 Long Term Experimental Management Plan (LTEMP) EIS and ROD reviewed and synthesized more than two decades of scientific study, and generally supported the adaptive management approach. The LTEMP accepted the previously authorized desired future conitions (DFCs) for the river corridor,[1] and confirmed triggering criteria for experimental high flows to improve management of the Canyon's sand budget.[198, 309] The DFCs include consideration of the river ecosystem, cultural values, hydroelectric power production, and recreation, and are consistent with the directives of the 1992 Grand Canyon Protection Act. Approved triggering criteria for high flows allows for rapid response management of tributary-derived sand inputs.

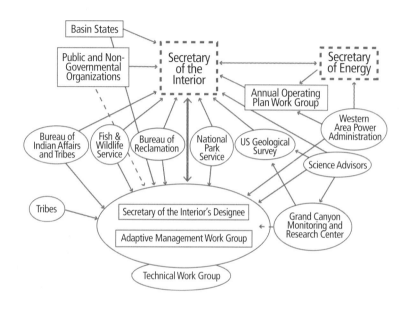

Fig. 6.5
Administrative structure of the Glen Canyon Dam Adaptive Management Program, lead by the US Bureau of Reclamation and reauthorized through the 2016 LTEMP ROD (modified [301]).

Colorado River Conservation in the 21st Century

Humans simplify the ecosystems around them to ensure safe, easy resource acquisition. We eliminate large predators and other organisms that compete with, or threaten us. We change the environment around us too quickly for the rest of life to keep up and lose additional species through collateral extinction. But along down the road of history come St. Francis, Henry Thoreau, John Muir, Theodore Roosevelt, Aldo Leopold, Rachael Carson, David Brower, and E. O. Wilson encouraging us to consider "existence rights"—that other life forms deserve respect, protection, and restoration for the benefit of nature and our own human well-being.

I am often asked, "Why not just decommission or remove Glen Canyon Dam—wouldn't that solve all these environmental problems?" The simple answer is "Probably not." Like youth, the pristine condition of the pre-dam CRE cannot be recovered. The existence and operations of Glen Canyon Dam have created an altered downstream ecosystem that now supports a somewhat different but remarkably robust aquatic-riparian ecosystem. Riparian zones have been decimated theoughout the West but the dam accidentally created 300 miles of shoreline habitat. Clear water and the novel profusion of shoreline vegetation support a rich allay of aquatic and riparian flora and invertebrates. These, in turn, support numerous breeding bird species, hundreds of migrants, a host of terrestrial vertebrates, and top predators like Peregrine Falcons, Bald Eagles, and an occasional Mountain Lion (*Puma concolor cougar*). The dam and its constantly cold water now protect remaining native fish species by keeping upstream non-native fish, fish diseases, crayfish, and other invertebrates out of Grand Canyon. The results of the Year 2000 flow regime, a $35 million ecosystem experiment, demonstrated that constant summer flows do not foster native fish recruitment, but do promote expansion of non-native species.[235] We cannot quickly restore the river to its pre-dam condition. Such a reversion requires careful study, planning, and execution.

So then, how can we manage the river ecosystem with the dam? Climate change predictions rather clearly indicate increased air temperature,[300] but the greatest concern is the prospect of prolonged drought.[314] The Bureau of Reclamation predicts that climate change-related failure of the water delivery system over the next 50 years may be a few percent at Glen Canyon Dam, but up to 19% of the time downstream at Hoover Dam.[300]

Another proposal to balance the ecology and economics of southwestern water management is the Glen Canyon Institute's "Fill Mead First" initiative. It proposes to designate Lake Mead as the primary water storage and distribution facility for both the upper and lower Colorado River basins.[161] By changing Glen Canyon Dam operations, Colorado River water could still be used to generate hydropower, but for the purpose of filling Lake Mead reservoir prior to filling Lake Powell. Rather than striving for a full pool (3,715 ft, 1,132 m) for Lake Powell, the reservoir's target elevation would be reset to 3,490 ft (1,064 m), allowing flood control, sediment conservation, reservoir-based recreation, some hydropower generation, and a proposed more natural water flow regime. However, such a plan would limit planned flood releases to retain sediment (because of insufficient head to run higher flows), increase water temperatures and plankton inflow into the river that may further threaten native fish, and generally further reduce flow variability of the CRE. Nonetheless, a more complete analysis of these and related ideas is warranted, particularly in light of pending climate-related water deficits, increasing demand, and pending revision of dam management plans.

Working to improve river ecosystem stewardship (see sidebar) in a region as complex as Grand Canyon means first understanding how much we don't understand. Helping improve river stewardship is open to all of us, thanks to former President Richard Nixon's Federal Advisory Committee Act, Endangered Species Act, National Environmental Policy Act, Clean Air Act, Clean Water Act, and other legislation. But it is up to each of us to avail ourselves of the democratic opportunities with which we have been blessed. Please attend AMWG meetings, keep writing letters to your public officials, and keep working for an intact, well-protected Grand Canyon, and for a healthy Earth. But get out for a river adventure just as often as you can!

Current Threats

The ecological integrity of Grand Canyon is threatened by a number of developments and social challenges. These include: expansion of development on the South Rim that threatens Grand Canyon groundwater, air quality, and dark sky resources; more than 3,000 uranium mining claims on the rim lands around Grand Canyon; the Escalade gondola project with development on the Navajo Nation rim near the Little Colorado River confluence; an erupting non-native beefalo herd on the North Rim; and pending non-native species invasion by quagga mussel, green sunfish, brown trout, and other species in the river corridor.

Stewardship Recommendations

Eternal vigilance is the cost of environmental and social justice.

1. Use the dam to protect native species and natural ecosystem processes, and respect economic values.

2. Respect and integrate indigenous Tribal values in river and Canyon management.

3. Rigorously integrate unbiased science into innovative and responsive stewardship.

4. Use naturally-timed high flows to manage sandbars (November floods are not natural), and limit sand export during equalization.

5. Restore the range of Humpback Chub and other native fish to the Paria River mouth.

VII. RIVER RUNNER RESOURCES

Background Reading

For overviews of the enormous literature on Grand Canyon and the Colorado River, the following bibliographies are available:

A Bibliography of the Grand Canyon and the Lower Colorado River, grandcanyonbiblio.org.[260]

The Books of the Colorado River & Grand Canyon, Francis P. Farquar.[90a]

Other Grand Canyon River Guidebooks

Belknap's Waterproof Grand Canyon River Guide, Buzz Belknap and Loie Belknap Evans.[86]

A River Runner's Guide to the History of the Grand Canyon, Kim Crumbo.[61]

Fly Fishing Lees Ferry: The Complete Guide to Fishing and Boating the Colorado River Below Glen Canyon Dam, Dave Foster

Guide to the Colorado River in Grand Canyon, Tom Martin and Duwain Whitis.

Grand Canyon Map and Data Portal & River Flows

Maps & Data: U.S. Geological Survey Grand Canyon Monitoring and Research Center, www.gcmrc.gov

River flows: waterdata.usgs.gov

Commercial Grand Canyon River Outfitters

Commercial companies below are authorized by the National Park Service to provide 1–18 day trips in motorized rafts, oar and paddle boats, dories and customized chartered trips. The Grand Canyon River Outfitters Association (gcroa.org or 928-556-0669) is the trade organization of the commercial outfitters.

Aramark-Wilderness River Adventures, riveradventures.com, 800-992-8022

Arizona Raft Adventures, azraft.com; 800-786-RAFT

Arizona River Runners, raftarizona.com; 800-477-7238

Canyon Explorations/Canyon Expeditions, canyonexplorations.com, 800-654-0723

Canyoneers, canyoneers.com; 800-525-0924

Colorado River and Trail Expeditions, crateinc.com, 800-253-7328

Grand Canyon Discovery, grandcanyondiscovery.com, 800-786-RAFT

Grand Canyon Dories, oars.com/grandcanyon/dories, 800-346-6277

Grand Canyon Expeditions Company, gcex.com; 800-544-2691

Grand Canyon Whitewater, grandcanyonwhitewater.com, 800-343-3121

Hatch River Expeditions, hatchriverexpeditions.com, 800-856-8966

Hualapai River Runners, grandcanyonwest.com, 888-868-9378

Moki Mac River Expeditions, mokimac.com, 800-284-7280

O.A.R.S., oars.com, 800-346-6277

Outdoors Unlimited, outdoorsunlimited.com, 800-637-7238

Tour West, twriver.com, 800-453-9107

Western River Expeditions, westernriver.com, 800-453-7450

Colorado River Discovery, raftthecanyon.com, 888-522-6644

Fishing Guides at Lees Ferry

Bailey's Custom Fishing, baileyscustomfishing.com, 928-699-2837

Lake Powell Outfitters, leesferryfishing.com, 928-640-2211

Lees Ferry Anglers, leesferry.com, 800-962-9755

Marble Canyon Outfitters, leesferryflyfishing.com, 800-533-7339

Northern Arizona Guide Service, leesferryguideservice.com, 928-719-1048

Grand Canyon Conservation and Educational Organizations / Information

Adaptive Management Work Group, http://gcdamp.com

Bureau of Reclamation, usbr.gov/uc/rm/amwg

Center for Biological Diversity, center@biologicaldiversity.org

Defenders of Wildlife, defenders.org

Grand Canyon Association, gcassociation@grandcanyon.org

Grand Canyon Historical Society, grandcanyonhistory.org

Grand Canyon Private Boaters Association, gcpba.org

Grand Canyon River Guides, gcrg.org

Grand Canyon River Outfitters Association. gcroa.org

Grand Canyon Trust, grandcanyontrust.org

Grand Canyon Wildlands, grandcanyonwildlands.org

Grand Canyon Youth, gcyouth.org

National Parks Conservation Association, npca@npca.org

River Runners for Wilderness, rrfw.org

Save The Confluence, savetheconfluence.com

The Sierra Club, sierraclub.org

Wildlands Network, wildlandsnetwork.org

Professional Outfitting & Shuttle Services for Private Trips

Canyon REO, canyonreo.com, 800-637-4604

Ceiba Adventures, ceibaadventures.com, 800-217-1060

Moenkopi Riverworks, moenkopiriverworks.com, 877-454-7483

Professional River Outfitters, proriver.com, 800-648-3236

River Runner Shuttle Service, rrshuttleservice.com, 928-564-2194

Private River Trips

Grand Canyon River Permits: The Park Service runs an annual weighted lottery in February for noncommercial permit dates for the following year. Go to the "River Trips/Permits" section at nps.gov/grca. The NPS website includes the launch calendar, noncommercial trip regulations, boating tips, river flow forecast links, planning videos, the Colorado River Management Plan and other invaluable information.

Diamond Creek to Lake Mead Permits: Permits for this reach are acquired through the National Park Service at: nps.gov/grca/planyourvisit/overview-diamond-ck.htm or 800-959-9164). Access to Diamond Creek is across Hualapai Tribe lands and requires advance payment of access fees. Call 928-769-2219 or 888-868-9378.

LEES FERRY AREA

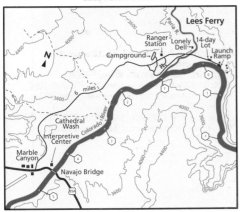

Lees Ferry (The Put-in)

Lees Ferry is the put-in for all full-length Grand Canyon river trips. Commercial, research, and private trips are nearly always rigging at Lees Ferry and space may be limited on the launch ramp. Please try to keep vehicles and equipment on designated parts of the ramp so as not to obstruct other parties.

If you have free time at Lees Ferry, there are several interesting explorations to undertake, including fishing, strolling around the Lonely Dell Ranch Historic Site (a short distance up the Paria River), or hiking up the nearby Spencer Trail, which climbs 1700 feet in two miles up a nearby ridge to spectacular views of Glen Canyon, Marble Canyon and the Vermilion Cliffs. (nps.gov/glca/planyourvisit/lees-ferry.htm).

Three lodges are located on Highway 89A 5–15 miles west of the Ferry. Marble Canyon Lodge (marblecanyoncompany.com, 800-726-1789) has gas, a post office, laundry mat, small store, motel and airstrip. The historic lodge building housing the restaurant and bookstore was destroyed in a fire in 2013, but will be restored by autumm 2014. Lees Ferry Lodge at Vermilion Cliffs (vermilioncliffs.com, 928-355-2231) is a down-home bar and restaurant with good accommodations and a great selection of beer. Cliff Dwellers Lodge (cliffdwellerslodge.com, 800-962-9755) offers a good restaurant, small convenience store, fly fishing and outfitters shop, fishing boat rentals, gas, lodging and airstrip.

Commercial airline service is available 50 miles away in Page, Arizona, the largest town on the Arizona Strip. It offers a wider selection of lodging, restaurants, shopping and medical services, as well as the Powell Museum (powellmuseum.org, 888-597-6873).

The Navajo Bridge Interpretive Center (nps.gov/glca/historyculture/navajobridge) 4 miles south of Lees Ferry has exhibits, a bookstore, good views of California Condors, and a scenic stroll across the historic 1929 bridge.

Downriver Camps: Courtesy and Karma

Paradise is crowded, and it is important for all of us to work towards friendly, diplomatic communications. There are relatively few camps in the narrower reaches of the river, including between Miles 9–39 in Marble Canyon, Miles 76–117 in the Inner Gorge, Miles 140–165 in the Havasu area, and Miles 226–270 below Diamond Creek. Make a point of talking with all the trips you meet about where you and they intend to camp.

Some of the beaches in the Canyon are camped at nearly every night during the summer months. This is a lot of use for some delicate sites. Those of us who love the Canyon hate to see signs of toilet paper, fire scars, and careless camping practices. Go out of your way to pick up that cigarette butt or micro-litter on the beach—honor the place.

Phantom Ranch

Located a quarter mile up Bright Angel Creek near Mile 88R, Phantom Ranch is accessible by mule, on foot or by river. It is an oasis of civilization at the bottom of the Grand Canyon. Some choose to purposely avoid it, but others enjoy exploring its historical buildings, or cooling off in Bright Angel Creek. At Phantom Ranch you will find rustic cabins, a hiker's campground, and a canteen with excellent lemonade and various sundries. Postcards and letters are still delivered to/from Phantom Ranch, but packages are no longer accepted. Send mail to: (recipient's name), Phantom Ranch River Runners Mail, c/o Grand Canyon National Park, PO Box 1266, Grand Canyon, AZ 86023.

For lodging at Phantom Ranch and the South Rim, and mule rides and duffel delivery services information, contact: grandcanyonlodges.com or 888-297-2757.

Havasupai Lodge

The Havasupai Tribe (928-448-2121; theofficialhavasupaitribe.com) operates the Havasupai Lodge (928-448-2111) in Havasu Canyon at Supai, AZ.

Diamond Creek (Put-in/Take-out)

The take-out is at Mile 226L, just upstream from the mouth of Diamond Creek. The Diamond Creek Road follows the stream bed and is subject to frequent flash-flooding and closure, particularly from July through September. The Hualapai Tribe requests that river trips take out after their daily trips launch at 10:00 a.m. The road and take-out are on Hualapai Tribe lands and require payment of access fees in advance to the Hualapai Tribe (888-868-9378). The Hualapai Lodge has a nice restaurant and rooms in Peach Springs (25 miles; about one hour from Diamond Creek, if the road is in good shape, 928-769-2230). Lodging and road food are available in Seligman and Kingman (both 55 miles and about 2.5 hours away from Diamond Creek).

Pearce Ferry and South Cove (take-outs)

The NPS has constructed a low-lake take-out at Pearce Ferry, several hundred yards upstream from Pearce Ferry Rapid. The rapid worsens considerably at lower lake levels, so don't miss the pull-in.

Hiking in/Hiking out

Several trails are commonly used for hiking into or out from river trips (see the following trail maps). However, such hikes are extremely rigorous, if not life-changing. These hikes should only be undertaken by those in good health, with thorough planning, adequate time, water, food, and secure logistics. For more information on these and other trails, see nps.gov/grca and several excellent hiking guidebooks.[40, 292, 334a]

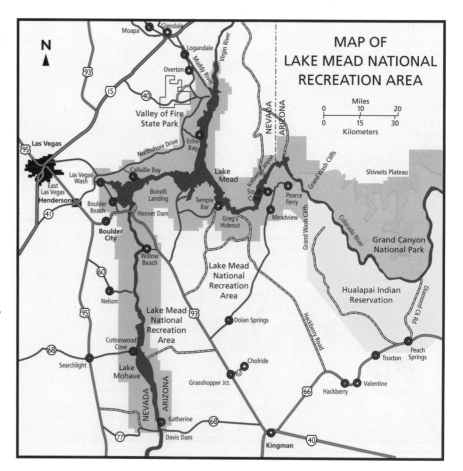

MAP OF
LAKE MEAD NATIONAL
RECREATION AREA

Tanner Trail

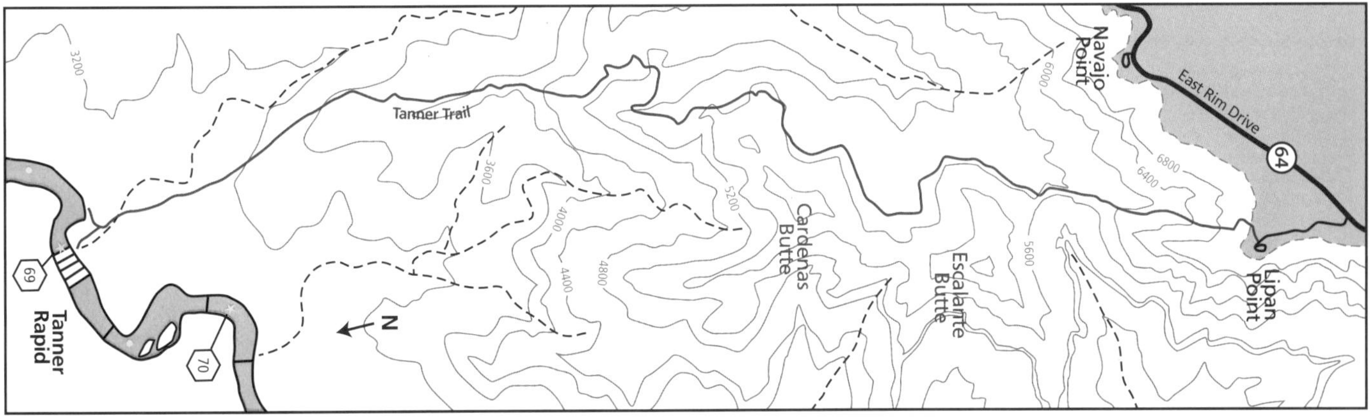
Navajo Point
East Rim Drive
64
Tanner Trail
3200
3600
4000
4400
4800
5200
5600
6000
6400
6800
Cardenas Butte
Escalante Butte
Lipan Point
Tanner Rapid
69
70
N

South Kaibab Trail

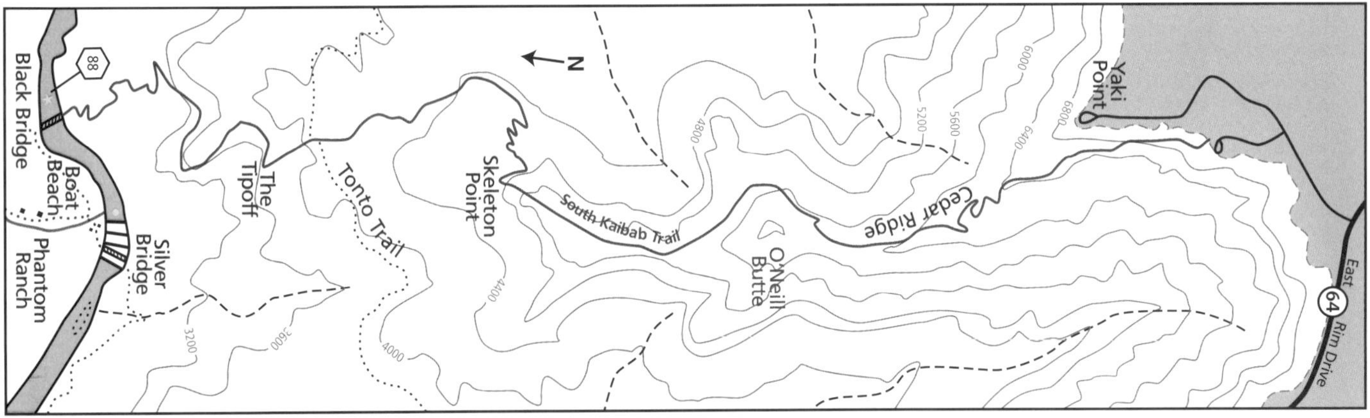
88
Black Bridge
Boat Beach
Silver Bridge
Phantom Ranch
The Tipoff
Tonto Trail
Skeleton Point
South Kaibab Trail
Cedar Ridge
O'Neill Butte
Yaki Point
East Rim Drive
64
N
3200
3600
4000
4400
4800
5200
5600
6000
6400
6800

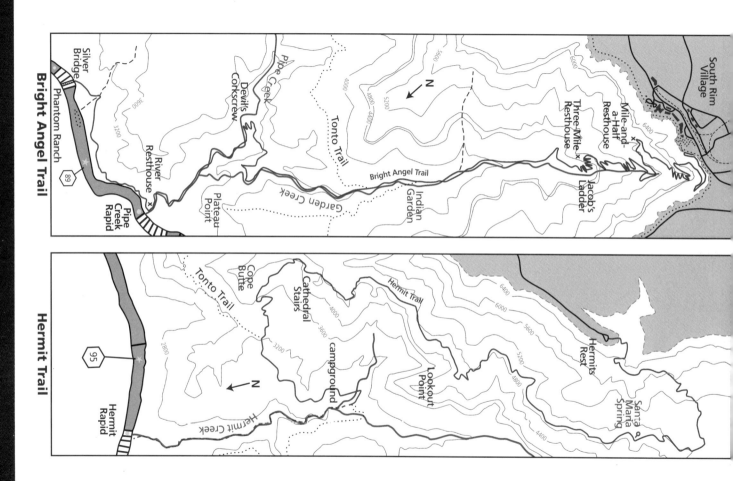

Bright Angel Trail

Silver Bridge
Phantom Ranch
89
Pipe Creek Rapid
River Resthouse
Devils Corkscrew
Pipe Creek
Plateau Point
Tonto Trail
Garden Creek
Indian Garden
Bright Angel Trail
Three-Mile Resthouse
Mile-and-a-Half Resthouse
Jacob's Ladder
South Rim Village
N
3600
3200
4000
5200
4800
4400
5600
6000
6400

Hermit Trail

95
Hermit Rapid
Tonto Trail
Cope Butte
Cathedral Stairs
campground
Hermit Creek
Lookout Point
Hermit Trail
Hermit's Rest
Santa Marta Spring
N
2800
3200
3600
4000
4400
4800
5200
5600
6000
6400

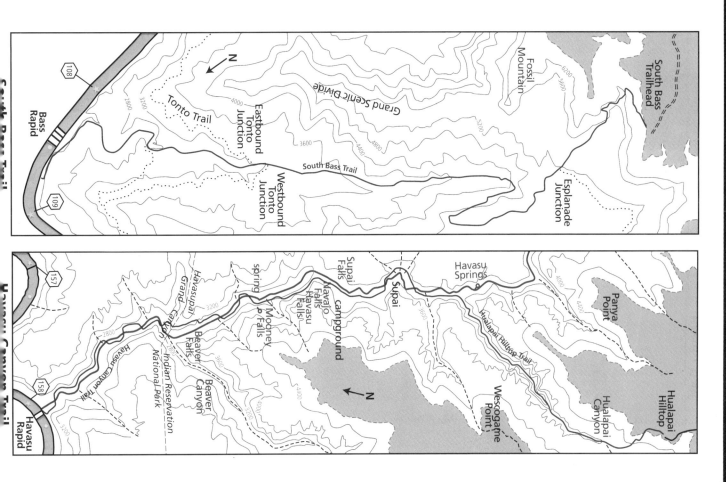

108

Bass
Rapid

109

N

3200
2800
4000
Tonto Trail

Eastbound
Tonto
Junction

Westbound
Tonto
Junction

3600

South Bass Trail

4400
4800

5200

5600
6200

Grand Scenic Divide

Fossil
Mountain

South Bass
Trailhead

Esplanade
Junction

157

158

Havasu
Rapid

3200
2800

3200

3600

Havasu Canyon Trail

Indian Reservation
National Park

Havasupai
Grand Canyon

Beaver
Falls

Beaver
Canyon

spring

Mooney
Falls

Navajo
Falls

Havasu
Falls

Supai
Falls

4000
3600

4400

N

campground

Supai

Havasu Springs

Wescogame
Point

Hualapai Hilltop Trail

4000

4400

Panya
Point

Hualapai
Canyon

Hualapai
Hilltop

INDEX

adaptive ecosystem management: 132
Adaptive Management Working Group
(AMWG): 93, 132, 133, 135, Figure 6.5
-- 133
Airline Overflight Act: 93
Alpine Tundra Zone: 99
amphibians: 108, 109, 120, Plate 5F -- 120,
Table 5.2 -- 109
Anasazi Bridge: 102
animals: (see fauna)
aquatic domain: 101; productivity 102
aspect: 102, 103
banded iron deposits: 71
basalt: 85
Bass, William W.: 90
Beamer, Ben: 89
beaver: 113, Table 5.4 -- 112
Belknap, Buzz: 92
Burg, Amos: 92
bibliographies: 136
Big Bang: 69
biogenesis: 69
biogeography: 99-101
biology: Chapter 5; 97-120
biomes: 98
birds: 111, 113 Table 5.3 -- 110
Birdseye, Claude: 91
biting flies: 106
Boucher, Louis: 90
Bridge Canyon Dam: 95
Bright Angel (Silver) Bridge: 92
Bright Angel Trail: map -- 140
Brower, David: 95
Bureau of Reclamation: 124
California Condor: 99

California River: 82
Canadian Zone: 99
canyons - other large: 67
Cárdenas, Garcia Lopez de: 87, 88
chert: 76
Clark, Georgie: 92
climate change: 65
Colorado Pikeminnow: 100
Colorado Plateau: 55, map 56
Colorado River Compact (1922): 122, Table
6.1 -- 123
Colorado River Ecosystem: dam changes
125, 132
Colorado River ecosystem (CRE): 101
Colorado River flows at Lees Ferry: annual
127, post-dam 127, pre-dam 127
Colorado River Management Plan: 93
Colorado River Storage Project Act (1956):
92, 95; Table 6.1 -- 123
Colorado River: antecedence, anteposition,
overflow, superimposition 84; course
57-58, 86; depth 57;
development 81, 84; sediment transport 86;
source 55
commercial Grand Canyon outfitters: 136
conservation: 134, 135; organizations 136
conservation history (Grand Canyon): 94-96
Daggett and Beer swimming expedition: 92
Darling, Ding: 95
de Colmot, Genevieve: 92
debris fan-eddy complex: 60-61
desert varnish: 76
Desert View Watchtower: 91
desired future conditions: Table 6.1 -- 123
Devonian river channel: 75
Diamond Creek: put-in/take-out: 138
camps: 137

drainage reversal: 82
Dutton, Clarence: 80
ecology: 97
Eddy, Clyde: 91
eon (geologic): 70, Archean 70, Hadean 69,
Phanerozoic 71, Proterozoic 70; Table
3.1 -- 70
era (geologic): Cenozoic 81-84;
Mesoproterozoic 70; Mesozoic 77, 82;
Neoproterozoic/Precambrian
74; Paleoproterozoic 70; Paleozoic 74-75;
Table 3.1 -- 70
Farlee Hotel: 90
fault: 80; Bright Angel 74; Butte 74;
Eminence 86; Hurricane 83
fauna: 105-107
Fill Mead First initiative: 135
fish: 107, 114, Plate 5E -- 119, Table 5.1
-- 107
fishing guides at Lees Ferry: 136
Flavell and Montez trapping expedition: 90
floods: historic 83, 126; planned; see high
flow experiments
formations: 56, 68; Bass Limestone 73;
Bright Angel Shale 75; Cardenas Basalts
74; Carmel 77; Chinle 77; Coconino
Sandstone 76; Dakota Sandstone 77;
Dox 74; Elves Chasm Geniss 71; Entrada
77; Esplanade 76; Galeros 74; Granite
Gorge Metamorphic Suite 73; Hermit
Shale 76; Hotauta Conglomerate 73;
Kaibab 76, 80; Kayenta 77; Kwagunt
74; Manakacha 76; Moenave 77;
Moenkopi 77; Muav Limestone 75;
Muddy Creek 82; Nankoweap 74;
Navajo Sandstone 77; Redwall 75--76;
Shinarump Conglomerate 77; Shinumo

Quartzite 73; Sixtymile 74; Supai (group) 76; Surprise Canyon 76; Tapeats 75; Temple Butte 75; Toroweap 76; Undivided Dolomites 75; Vishnu Schist 71, 73; Watahomigi 76; Wescogame 76; Zoroaster Plutonic Complex (Granite) 73; Fig. 3.2 -- 72

fossils: 70, 74, 75, 76, 77

Fred Harvey: 91

Galloway, Nathaniel: 90

Garces, Francisco: 88

geography: Chapter 1, 55

geology: Chapter 3; definitions & concepts 68; erosion 68; geochronology 69; time 69-70; unconformities 68

Glen Canyon Dam: Chapter 6; Adaptive Management Working Group (AMWG) 132-133; construction of 83, 92; dedication 124; design 122, 124; history 121–124; impacts of 59; 121, 132; Table 6.1 -- 123

Glen Canyon Environmental Studies Program: 93

Glen Canyon National Recreation Area: 124

Grand Canyon: 55; age 67; area 56; basins 58-59; depth 67; geologic evolution 80; volume 57

Grand Canyon (pink) Rattlesnake: 100

Grand Canyon Forest Reserve: 94

Grand Canyon Monitoring & Research Center: 133

Grand Canyon National Monument: 94, 95

Grand Canyon National Park: 91, 95, 121

Grand Canyon N.P. Enlargement Act: 93

Grand Canyon Protection Act (1992): 93, 121, Table 6.1 -- 123, 133

Grand Canyon Wildlands: 7, 96

Grand Wash: 58, 86

Grant, Zee: 92

Great American Interchange: 83

Great Basin Desert: 98

Great Denudation: 80

group (geology): Grand Canyon 71, 73; San Rafael 77; Supai 76; supergroup (geologic) 68; Tonto 75; Unkar 73

Gulf of California: 83

Hance, Cpt. John: 90

Havasu Canyon trail: map -- 141

Hermit Trail: map -- 140

High Flow Experiment (Planned Flood): 93, 128, 129, 133

hiking in/hiking out: 138-141

Holmstrom, Buzz: 92

Honeymoon Couple: 91

Hoover Dam: 66, 83, 122

Hudson, Marstron and Taylor expedition: 92

Hudsonian Zone: 99

human history: Chapter 4; 87-96

Humpback Chub: 1, 107, 108, 119, Plate 5E -- 119, Table 5.1 -- 107

invertebrates: 105-106; aquatic 106; Plate 5D -- 118

Ives, Joseph C.: 5, 89

Johnson, Lyndon B.: 95, 96

Kaibab Fmn, Limestone: 55

Kanab Ambersnail: 101

kinematic wave: 125, Figure 6.1 -- 125

Kolb brothers: 91

Kruger and Landick canoe up-run: 93

La Rue, E.C.: 91

Lake Mead National Recreation Area: map -- 138

lava (see basalt): 84-85

Lava Falls Volcanic Field: 84-85

Law of the River: 122

Lee Ferry: 91, 122

Lee, John D.: 89

Lees Ferry: 66, 102; flow Figs 6.2-6.4 -- 127, map -- 137, put-in 137

legislation: 121–124, 133, Table 6.1 -- 123

Leuchochloridium snail parasite: 101

Litton, Martin: Map mile 194

lizards: 109, 111, 120, Plate 5F -- 120, Table 5.2 -- 109

Long Term Experimental Management Plan (LTEMP): 93, 132–133

Lower Sonoran Zone: 99

mammals: 113, Table 5.4 -- 112

Marble Canyon Dam: 95

Marble Canyon National Monument: 92

Merriam, C. Hart: 97

Mexican Hat Expeditions: 92

mining: 96

modified low, fluctuating flows (MLFF) flow regime: 132

Mohave Desert: 58, 98

Mountain Meadows Massacre: 89

Muav Gorge: 59

Native Americans: Chapter 4, 83, 87-93; Anasazi 87; Archaic 87; Athabaskan 88; Cohonina 87; Formative 87; Hopi 87; Havasupai 87; Hisatsinom 87; Hualapai 87; Navajo 87, 88; Pai 87; Paiute 87; Paleoindian 87; Preformative 87; Uto-Aztecan 87; Fig. 4.1 -- 87; Fig. 4.2 -- 89

Navajo Bridge: 91

Nevills, Norman: 92

New Zealand Mudsnail: 97

non-native species: 97

Nutter, Preston: 90

O'Neill, Buckey: 90, 93

orogeny (geologic): Basin and Range 82; Laramide 82

Oxygen Catastrophe: 70

paleogeography: 78-79

Pangea: 70; 77; 79

Paria River: 55, 102

Pattie, James O.: 55, 88

Pearce (Pierce), Harrison: Ferry 89

Pearce Ferry: take-out 138

Peregrine Falcon: 113

period (geologic): 70; Cambrian 75; Carboniferous 75-76; Cretaceous 77; Cryogenic 74; Devonian 75; Ediacaran 74; Jurassic 77; Mississipian 75-76; Neogene 70; Ordovician 75; Paleogene 70; Paleoproterozoic 70; Pennsylvanian 76; Permian 76-77; Silurian 75; Triassic 77; Table 3.3.1 -- 70

Phantom Ranch: 91, 137

plant species: Plates 5A–C, 103

plate tectonics: 79, 84

post-dam: aquatic domain 130, comparison with pre-dam 126, flows 126, rapids 129, riparian zone 131, sedimentology 128, water temperature 129

Powell, John Wesley: 6, 81, 88, 89

precipitation: 63

pre-dam: aquatic domain 130, comparison with post-dam 126, flows 126, rapids 129, riparian zone 130, sedimentology 128, water temperature 129

private river trips: 137

put-in: Diamond Creek 138, Lees Ferry 137

Quagga Mussel: 97

railroads: 90, 93

rapids: 58–60

Razorback Sucker: 114, 119, Plate 5E -- 119, Table 5.1 -- 107

reaches (geomorphic): geomorphic 59-60; Table 1.1

regression (marine): 75

reptiles: 108, 109, 120, Plate 5F -- 120, Table 5.2 -- 109

Rigg, Jim and Bob: 92

ringtails: 113, 114, Table 5.4 -- 112

riparian domain: 101; habitats 60

river miles: 7, 56

river runner resources: 136

Roosevelt, Theodore: 90, 94

Russell and Monet expedition: 90

Russell, Tadje & Clements expedition: 91

Rust, David: 90

sandbar loss: 128, see high flow experiment

Sanger, King, Wooley expedition: 90

scud (Gammarus): 106

sedimentology: 128

shuttle services: 137

Sierra Club: 95

slump (slope failure): 83

snakes: 109, 111, Plate 5F -- 120, Table 5.2 -- 109

snow: 64

snowball Earth: 74

Sonoran Desert: 58. 98

Sonoran River Otter: 114

South Bass Trail: map -- 141

South Cove: take-out 138

South Kaibab Trail: map -- 139

Southwestern Willow Flycatcher: 113

Speckled Rattlesnake: 45, 100

Spencer, Charles: 91

Stanton, Robert B.: 90

stewardship: 135

strata (see formation):

supercontinent: 79; Pangaea 77

take-out: Diamond Creek 138, Pearce Ferry and South Cove 138

Tamarisk (Salt-cedar): 104, 113; leaf beetle 113

Tanner Trail: map -- 139

Tanner, Seth: 89

Tarantual ahwk: 105

temperature: air 63

Transition Zone: 99

tributaries: 58, 101

trout: 107, Table 5-1 -- 107

turbidity segments: 59

turtles: 111, Table 5.2 -- 109

unconformity: 68; Great 74; Pre-Devonian 75

Upper Sonoran Zone: 99

uranium mines: 96

vegetation: 103-104; riparian 103; tributaries 104; vegetation change 131; zonation 104

velvet ant: 105

waif species: 100

Waltenberg, John; 91, Map mile 113

water supply: 65

weather: fall 64, fog 66, humidity 66, spring 63, snow 64, summer 63, wind 65, winter 64

Wegner, David L.: 93

Western Area Power Administration: 124

Western Diamonback Rattlesnake: 100

Western Water Law: 122

White, James: 89

wind: 65

Year 2000 flow regime: 134